CONTENTS

Trust

ADRIAAN T. PEPERZAK

Trust

WHO OR WHAT MIGHT SUPPORT US?

Fordham University Press
New York 2013

Library of Congress Cataloging-in-Publication Data

Peperzak, Adriaan Theodoor, 1929–
Trust : who or what might support us? / Adriaan T. Peperzak. — First edition.
p. cm
Includes bibliographical references and index.
ISBN 978-0-8232-4488-1 (cloth : alk. paper) —
ISBN 978-0-8232-4489-8 (pbk. : alk. paper)
1. Trust. 2. Trust—Religious aspects. 3. Religion—Philosophy. I. Title.
BJ1500.T78P46 2013
179'.9—dc23

2012043870

Printed in the United States of America
15 14 13 5 4 3 2 1
First edition

INSTEAD OF A PREFACE

How should we live?
Whose guidance can we trust?

Be yourself!
Act responsibly!

Can I trust myself?
Nature? Humanity? History?

Follow us!
Who are you?

Distrust the loudest!
Trust the genuine!

Show me trusting and trustworthy lives!
But first, what does it mean: to trust?

ACKNOWLEDGMENTS

I am grateful to the Templeton Foundation for the grant that made this book possible, and I thank Professor Robert Crease both for his kind invitation to give a series of lectures on trust at Stony Brook University and for the perfect hospitality with which he welcomed me to the department of philosophy he chairs. I want to include in my gratitude Ms. Alissa Betz and Ms. Ann Marie Monaghan, who gracefully managed my visits, the colleagues who participated in our meetings, and the students who attended the seminar on Heidegger's *Being and Time,* which took place on the same days as our discussions on trust and distrust.

I am deeply aware that I cannot thank enough all those good persons who—as teachers, writers, students, colleagues, friends, managers, or sympathizers—have made this book possible. Although this book does not contain discussions with the many authors whose writings have nourished my reflections on trust, I want to mention one of them, Joseph J. Godfrey, with special gratitude for having allowed me to read his encompassing and very helpful manuscript whose final version has been published recently as *Trust of People, Words, and God: A Route for Philosophy of Religion* (Notre Dame, Ind.: Notre Dame University Press, 2012).

I want to address a very special "Thank you!" to Stacy Bautista and Giancarlo Tarantino for their wonderful and generous cooperation in the mental and material production of the present text.

What I owe to Angela for supporting me while spending time and attention on this book, however, surpasses too much what can be said in public; she knows how grateful I am for her role in my trust.

Introduction

I began writing this book when Professor Robert Crease, chairman of NYU's Department of Philosophy at Stony Brook, sent me an invitation to give a series of lectures on trust as part of a Templeton grant for research and discussion on *The Relevance of Trust from the Perspective of the Relations between Religion and the Sciences.* On March 16, 2009, the first lecture was delivered and discussed with an interdisciplinary group of colleagues. Five other lectures and discussions followed in March and April of that year. However, the completion of this book had to be postponed until the summer of 2010, while reviewing and additional editing took about a year. To contextualize the questions that are emphasized in this book, I sketch here briefly, while using words of my introductory lecture, how I understood the *task* that was implied in the grant and the *situation* in which I tried to do my part in its execution.

Several elements of the proposed topic deserve emphasis and preliminary observation before we can concentrate on a direct answer to the questions implied in it. We cannot begin an examination of the triangle religion-science-trust, for example, unless we rely on an already available, albeit naïve and possibly deficient, acquaintance with the meaning and functioning of several phenomena evoked by the word *trust* and some of its cognates. The fact that we come together "in the name of trust" shows that each of us has such an acquaintance. That all of us share exactly the same understanding of "trust" or "distrust," however, is *not* certain, but it is safe to state that our meeting by itself testifies to a common interest that seems to be indicated directly or indirectly by those words.

A second feature of our encounter is the assumption that we, as professionals of various academic disciplines, are together sufficiently competent to conduct a scholarly discussion about the meaning and the relevance of trust from a perspective that does not only include those disciplines but also *religion.*

Since all scholarly knowledge emerges from prescholarly acquaintance with important phenomena that we, as human beings, have experienced before we ascended to the level of science or philosophy and still experience outside the domain of our strictly professional activities, we must pay attention to the relations between our naïve acquaintance with trust and our scholarly-conducted investigations of it. This observation is particularly urgent when an examination concerns a phenomenon that cannot entirely be studied from the outside, because the examiners themselves are constantly involved in its practice. In the present case this means that we are engaged in trusting one another as contributors to a conversation, while at the same time wanting to be involved in a rigorous investigation about trust, without, if possible, allowing private biases to prevail over a truthful approach.

As far as my own competence—and, I fear, some biases—are concerned, my contribution will not only be philosophical rather than scientific, but even more limited than the predicate "philosophical" might suggest. Indeed, I am at home in a philosophical tradition that British philosophers began to call "continental" when they said farewell to their longstanding veneration of Hegel and other luminaries of the European continent, in order to unite in a trend they proudly baptized "analytic philosophy" (as if Hegel were too hasty in forging syntheses or too lazy in making distinctions). The fact that someone who has enjoyed working in both Hegelian and post-Husserlian phenomenology was asked to write this book has given me the courage to interpret Templeton's formulation of the task in a generous sense, which includes philosophy among the epistemic and meta-scientific approaches to the sciences and religion.

OBJECTIVE AND LITERATURE

The philosophical literature on trust is not huge, if one sticks to a narrow meaning of the word *trust.* Sociology and psychology have been more productive. But related subjects, such as hope, faith, expectation, confidence, fidelity, and promise have been regularly studied from Parmenides onward, down to our own time. And yet, it is not easy to assemble and integrate the available thoughts and suggestions into a not only analytic but also synthetic treatise. The existing literature in the social sciences, offers a host of interesting analyses, which offer a philosopher much food for thought. This book has profited from that literature; but one might recognize more allusions to philosophical classics in it. Because the book is meant for a broader audience than that of specialists, however, the use of explicit references and quotations has been restricted to an absolute minimum.

The selection of questions concerning trust and distrust begins with an introductory description of trust, which emphasizes its belonging to a particular class of interpersonal relations (chapter 1). Chapter 2 narrows the given description by analyzing the structure of someone's entrusting another individual with a certain activity. Expansions of that structure can be studied by focusing on someone's trust in certain features or segments of the society (chapter 3) and each person's own self-confidence (chapter 5). In chapter 4 I address the question: To what extent can we also trust the impersonal reality of nature and the material universe in which we live? Since this universe has become a humanized form of nature, we must—at least briefly—meditate on the enormous role the cosmos and its human transformations play in our corporeal and spiritual maturation. This meditation leads us to the most profound question concerning trust and distrust: Is a radical, at once basic and ultimate, trust possible with regard to our existence in this universe? In order to prepare an adequate formulation of this question and some of the answers it has received within the limits of our civilization, one must sketch the framework within which the question has been approached by the classics of modern philosophy (chapter 6) and by their predecessors, who practiced philosophy in close connection with their religious convictions (chapter 7). Chapter 8 then offers a series of observations concerning the three orientations of trust and distrust that seem to attract most intellectuals of our epoch: atheism, religious faith, and agnostic indecision.

SOME PRELIMINARY OBSERVATIONS

To set the tone for the method and the style that are adopted in the following chapters, a few observations might be helpful.

As my point of departure, I take it for granted that no human life has grown up without any trust and that no adult life is possible in its total absence. Trust emerges as soon as a child becomes aware of its dependence on parents, teachers, shopkeepers, friends, and so on. Perhaps the same may be said of distrust, insofar as children also discover that their wants do not necessarily square with the action plans of others. Trusting never ends, even for the most powerful, rich, smart, or wise. We trust the food we eat, the language we speak, the regularities that govern nature, most of the teachings of our teachers, the research of our colleagues, the systems that channel our communication. Exceptions that shock our trust make us cautious or—if the situation gets corrupt—suspicious, but even corruption has a tendency to establish its own rules so that our distrust can calculate the chances of obtaining more or less reliable outcomes.

Trust, accompanied by subordinate measures of distrust, conditions all the dimensions of our lives: in the first place our interpersonal dealings, to begin with those who have been most responsible for our birth, survival, and acculturation. Our entire formation—learning how to walk, speak, behave, remember, trust and distrust, and so on—relies on it. Formation is never finished, however; even the greatest genius needs reliable news, instruction, and exemplary models to remain up to date. All academic and scholarly work would stop if we could not count at all on the trustworthiness of predecessors, colleagues, and much of the available literature.

Intersubjective trust is, of course, a fascinating topic, especially for philosophers who have been educated in a climate where the self-conscious mind of rational egos plays a leading part. In order to reevaluate this climate, it might be worthwhile to examine the kinds of trust that connect today's people with one another. How are average Americans of all ages—including shopkeepers, intellectuals, scholars, scientists, philosophers, ministers, politicians, traders, and financial advisers—related in trust and distrust towards one another, the social institutions of their surrounding, and the various communities to which they belong? We should not neglect the fact that trust does not only connect singular persons, but also covers many anonymous elements of our environment. These likewise dominate not only our existential needs, but also our professional participation in particular modes of consensus or dissent and in powerful traditions of morality, politics, and religion.

A certain knowledge about trust belongs to the wisdom of life itself. What I call here "wisdom" is an existential kind of elementary acquaintance, developed by life itself as it, while aging, has become more experienced in performing itself underneath our explicit awareness. Living our lives, while driven by the very life one not only has but is, implies counting on persons, forces, tools, structures, rules, and situations that, despite important changes, continue to channel, orient, guide, and produce possibilities and realizations of meaning. A basic—albeit still undetermined and vague—trust in the world and life itself conditions our modes of belonging to several dimensions of human existence. If we lacked all trust on the basic levels of life, we would fall back into a chaos without form, rule, measure, or direction. Total disorientation would be the result. Nothing could be planned, decided, chosen, or willed, because we could not count on anything stable. Nothing trustworthy would appear; human time itself would vanish because no past could be told and no planable future projected.

If we cannot count on any regularity, behavior and motivation are not even thinkable.

If we try to imagine a human world without any trust, we come close to the most intense and threatening horror that emerges from a confrontation with nothing at all. Martin Heidegger has tried to describe the absence of all that might offer us a stable hold on which we can count, and Levinas has described it under the name of "*il y a*" ("there is"), an almost-nothing that has neither contours, nor a purpose, sense, or meaning.[1] In the course of this book, we will have to ask whether the most basic level of trust can be found in our originary being-situated in (the possibility of) meaning as such, or whether such a trust is no more than an illusory hope, already refuted by some proof of its utter impossibility—for example, by death, as annihilation of the entire universe insofar as each mortal person is concerned. The questions that arise from a "reduction" of our existence to nothing—which, as consciousness of mortality tells us, is not a fiction—implies the question of life's proper meaning, and this question is tied to the meaning of religion. Is it possible that religion is not outdated but relevant, even today? Are we allowed, reasonably advised, perhaps even urged—not only by death, but more so by life itself—to put our overall and ultimate trust in gods, a god, Fate, Moira, or the one God-self?"[2]

PART I: Varieties of Trust and Distrust

The word *trust* has several meanings and it is closely related to such near-synonyms as confidence, reliance, belief, credence, faith, or conviction. Some studies on trust have paid careful attention to the sometimes subtle distinctions between the various phenomena that are named by those words. Belief and reliance have especially been associated with those aspects of trust that have to do with questions of cognition and truth. I will not try to repeat such very useful explorations; however, I will emphasize those aspects of trust that are relevant for the affective and practical side of human existence. Thus, most of the cognitive aspects will be left to the epistemological literature that has already been produced, whereas trust as a specific form of existential involvement will be underlined. To give an example, trust as counting on another's knowledge or veracity (and distrust as reaction to someone's supposed mendacity or ignorance) will not take center stage, but it will be recognized as an essential element of trust in someone's social and practical trustworthiness.

A second warning is necessary. Although trust is the main subject of this book, its contrast with distrust shall not be ignored. If distrust were the main topic, however, we would have written much more about suspicion, critique, refusal, and condemnation, and, in the process, would have cited many modern and postmodern critics. However, would these critics have given us also sufficient antidotes and inspiration for forms of a new, postcritical trust?

Chapters 1 and 2 sketch an initial structure that could be developed into a formal treatise or "logic" of trust, whereas the three chapters of part 2 focus on the more concrete realities that inspire trust or distrust.

ONE

Trust

The philosophical literature on trust is not abundant. One of the reasons might lie in the fact that trust cannot be displayed, observed, or presented as a thing. A second reason is that trust, as a peculiar relation between someone and a trusted person or impersonal reality (an institution or machine, for example) cannot be described as the relation between a subject and an object. Although trust certainly involves me in a relation with someone or something—thus involving me also in the trusted other's existence—this involvement cannot be reduced to an "objective" relation, if the word *object* indicates that a certain reality can be displayed or presented as something over there, showing up for a freestanding subject, who perceives it from a distance. A trusted reality cannot be characterized as a "direct object" in the accusative; its appearance shows more likeness with a *dative.*

A FIRST APPROACH

I use the word *dative* to indicate a particular relation of a human subject to some reality that cannot be described as lying over against or in front of the subject who looks at it or puts it there and treats it at will. *Dative* is a specific form of the more generic case commonly called *indirect object.* A dative relation occurs when, for example, I *give you* a book or when I *tell you* a story. However, the word *dative* should neither be understood in a very literal and narrow sense, as if it only signifies a donative—giving or granting—relation, nor in a very wide sense that makes it almost indistinguishable from all other relations between a subject and some other reality. In many languages, the distinction between a dative and an accusative or directly objective (or objectifying) relation, is clearly marked by different cases. It is very important for an accurate phenomenology of a particular class of rapports without which no one can live. In this and the next chapter, I will attempt to clarify several properties of the dative structure and the effects it has on the person and things that are involved in it. This chapter introduces trust as one of the activities that have a dative structure, without insisting on the differences between trusting persons and trusting anonymous realities, such as tools, things, food, plants, the elements, meteorites, and so on. Chapter 2 will give an elementary analysis of the way in which the general structure of trusting another person is concretized in the phenomenon of entrusting, whereas chapters 3 through 5 extend our consideration to other realities and domains, including impersonal and inanimate ones. Thereby it will become apparent how involvement in relations of trust affects the trusting and the trusted parties in their modes of being. The relevance of trust for the performance of human existence will thus become obvious.

Before I try to distinguish and classify various kinds of trusting and being trusted, however, let us start with a simple example. When I trust you, this does not mean that I observe, study, analyze, manipulate, or contemplate you from a freestanding perspective or that I subject you to any plan or activity. Instead, by trusting you, I become involved in a kind of bonding with you. Trust creates a kind of participation between you and me, and this changes my life, including my feeling, working, and thinking, at least in some aspect and to a certain extent. My trust in you involves me in one or more aspects of your life and activity; it associates me with you and gives you a role in my way of dealing with the world. Consequently, your life becomes a part of my life, at least in certain respects. If, on the contrary, I distrust you, I will keep a cautious distance and protect myself against your interference.

When you are aware of my trust or distrust toward you, you hardly can avoid reacting to this fact. My attitude may influence your behavior, but you can, of course, refuse to get in contact with me. Such a refusal is then an answer, but a negative one. If you accept my trust, however, we are linked. This does not necessarily mean that you trust me—perhaps you don't—but you are then somehow related to me and a mutual involvement emerges, which contains an invitation to further exploration. Even if my confidence in you remains hidden to you, you—or, more accurately, that in you which I trust—has become a part of my existence. In a sense that must be examined more carefully, your way of experiencing or doing things becomes then also a part of my action and experience. In my existing and acting, I will count on you (your acting, making, thinking, feeling, writing, negotiating, speaking in my name, and so on). By trusting you with a part of my task, for example, I integrate a portion of your activities into my own activity.

My trust in you can be motivated in many ways. Perhaps I see in you certain skills that would help me to finish successfully a plan of my own, but it is also quite possible that your successful completion of a doctoral dissertation or the need of a third person is the main motif. "I trust you" can be motivated by many different considerations, but the trust relation itself has a relatively independent structure. What in any case seems clear is that your life, via my trust in you and your acceptance, overlaps with a part or aspect of my life and that our lives have become associated through a mutual bond that cannot be broken as long as trust connects our lives.

TURNING TO

To trust belongs to a class of verbs that indicate various kinds of *turning toward* someone or something, *without objectifying the intended reality.* Other examples are speaking or writing to someone, addressing, greeting, serving, or dedicating oneself to a person or something. All such verbs name a common structure, but one that differs from the structure of verbs like treating, producing, manipulating, determining, limiting, planning, studying, or similar verbs that express an objectifying or displaying and exposing activity. The difference between these two classes is analogous to the difference between *speaking to* and *speaking about.*

There are many ways of turning to someone: writing a letter to a friend, giving a gift, gesturing welcomingly, for example, but also joining or threatening someone or forbidding a person to do something. Probably most verbs followed by a dative preposition indicate a turning to someone who cannot be reduced to an objectifiable quality, function or thing.[1]

Can we trust not only persons, but also things or instruments? And can we trust ourselves, the government, the economic system, the world, history, humanity? Yes, but the structure of each variety of trust, and especially the particularity of our turning to a specific kind of reality (for example, while playing an instrument, confiding money to the bankers, voting for senators, and so on) must be analyzed each time anew, because the character of the relation between the trusting person and the trusted reality depends on the particular character of the latter and the perspective of the former's turn to it. At the beginning of this book it seems a safe bet to see the interpersonal trust as the main paradigm for our ulterior approach of other varieties, but we must check whether this hypothesis will be confirmed.

By turning (myself) toward someone, I join or bind myself to another person and this person to me (even if the other is not aware of it). The other concerns me then; he or she changes something in me by involving me in a personal relation with someone who then begins to play some—albeit tiny—role in my life. The result is that my position in the world changes because this other has become a part of my existence and consequently in some sense exists "for," "with," and even "in" me (or in and for my imagination, reflection, and memory). My existence would be different (differently turned, oriented, concerned)—I would stand and move differently—if the other's existence had not motivated me to turn to her. At the same time, my turn to another becomes part of my way of looking at the other.

Trusting someone does not only change me, but it also triggers a change in the other. If she is aware of my trust, she cannot avoid reacting to it—either by willingly ignoring or avoiding further contact, or by some form of reciprocal engagement. As stated earlier, this does not necessarily imply that she will trust me. It is, for example, possible that she wants to be hired by me for a confidential job because she needs a salary, although she has her doubts about me. If, on the contrary, she trusts me, the trust is mutual, even if its character on both sides may be very different. In this case, a double trusting changes two lives, insofar as these thereby get related in a particular way that modifies their positions in one shared world. It is certainly true that things, facts, and objects in which we are interested also can change my life by imposing their content on my awareness and actions, but insofar as they remain *objects,* their mode of entering into my life is not comparable to the kind of linking that is realized by trust. We must try to refine our understanding of the difference that is at stake. For starters, the question of whether one may expect reciprocal trust from pens, pianos, swimming pools, or medications, certainly sounds false—unless one's goal is to enter the realms of myths or fables.

A NOTE ON DISTRUST

If trust (or confidence) implies a positive kind of addressing or turning toward someone or something, we must ask in which sense *distrust* forms a contrast with it. Can distrust (or diffidence) be reduced to a kind of indifference, absence, neutrality, or impartiality, or does it take a characteristic stand, which, as contrasting with trust, is its negative correlate? Does distrust turn toward or away from a distrusted reality, but then in a distanced, reproving, or condemnatory way? Does it also constitute an aspect of the turn by which someone reacts or responds to someone else? And does it, too, become part of both the distrusting and the distrusted person's existence?

Although distrust would deserve a separate examination, a few provisional notes must suffice to show that it is not possible to define distrust by negating all the attributes that belong to trust.

When I receive information about someone who makes his trustworthiness regarding a specific assignment suspect to me, I will distrust his success. If a person is untrustworthy in many respects or overall—for example because he is a liar or imposter—I cannot but distrust him. The consequence is that I will avoid getting entangled in common enterprises with him, if these demand truthfulness. I will avoid confidential contacts, cautiously guard my words when I speak with him, and suppress personal information about other people and myself. Distrust that is generated by unreliability is clearly an obstacle for close relationships about important matters and frank cooperation.

If the person I distrust becomes aware of my suspicion, he might feel this fact unjustified. This may trigger anger, indifference, or the desire to prove me incorrect by clearing his name. Whatever he does, my distrust is not the right means to tighten cooperative or convivial ties between different people. Trust has a tendency to connect and unite, at least in some respects, whereas distrust causes dissociation and solitude. Too much distrust in a community prepares or expresses internal conflicts, but trust fosters agreement and internal peace. In this respect, trust is preferable over distrust; but the circumstances (for example, the generalized injustice of a totalitarian regime) may make naïve trust more pernicious than cautious distrust and intelligent lying.

KINDS OF TRUST

The elementary analysis of my trust in you, sketched in the preceding pages, must be expanded in several directions. With regard to the trusted, a complete analysis should also focus on him, her, us, you in the plural, them, and myself, and on a large number of impersonal realities, insofar as these are or can be trusted, whereas, on the side of the trusting persons the analysis would direct our attention to you, me, us, her, him, and all others who might put their confidence in a great diversity of trustworthy persons and things. This would then force us to examine (1) the characteristics of the relation between the two sides, as an each time particular union of trust and being trusted, and (2) the effects this relation causes in the parties involved. We would then see that such extensions of the structure found in "I trust you," cannot, without transformations, be transposed to other relations, in which I and you are replaced with different actors. Sentences such as "you trust her," "they put their trust in him," or "we trust (or distrust) them" need their own analyses to manifest the specific character of the relations expressed in them. This does not yet imply that we must disqualify our choice of an initial paradigm, but further analysis might make a revision of the adopted perspective necessary.

A further extension is necessary because we must also examine to what extent collective realities (such as communities, societies, nations) and nonhuman entities (such as dogs, birds, dolphins, elephants, or trees and orchids) can be trusted or may even show signs of their trust in us or other animals and instruments. Should we trust this cat, this snake, the roof on our house, the banks, the government, the idea of democracy, the capitalistic conception of freedom, the ecological changes that are proposed, our computer, my lungs, my heart? Does my dog, the IRS, the police, the nation, or the educational system trust me? Or must we use other words in order to formulate such questions more adequately? We can certainly investigate the authenticity of diamonds and the trustworthiness of the American democracy, and we can trust the efficiency of the French TGV, but does the trust that appears in such constellations bear a strong resemblance to the trust between you and me? Before we tackle such questions, however, let's first continue the analysis of our initial example, in order to acquire a more precise picture of at least one, not too complicated, model, which later can be relativized and modified.

YOU ARE TRUSTWORTHY

The sentence "I trust you" is incomplete, in the first place because trust always implies a purpose: I trust you with regard to some event or work that can or should be realized. For example, I trust that you will become a good teacher, a brilliant pianist, a loving spouse, a loyal associate; I trust that I may ask your help. I trust your sincerity, and so on.

Insofar as a certain goal must be achieved by you, I consider you trustworthy when I trust that you are capable and willing to achieve it. You have qualifications that justify my confidence in your success. From the perspective of the specific goal that must be realized, it is not necessary that I know more about you than that your skills fulfill the conditions for success and that you are dedicated to its realization. The rest of your life is here relevant only insofar as it would include impediments for a successful achievement. Your motivation, for example, can remain hidden. My trust is based on your relation to the purpose you probably will realize.

The relation between you and me becomes somewhat complicated, when I am the one who, as much as you, or even more, is interested in the work that you want to do; for example, because I have entrusted that work to you, who accepted this or asked for it. What has been said above remains then true, but the new element is that you and I want and will the same result; your will and mine share one particular purpose: the realization of one outcome that satisfies you and me. The only thing that both of us then agree on is the correct result of your performance. What we have in common is the coincidence of those aspects of our two wills that condition the one effect that both of us pursue. Such a coincidence can be realized despite deep differences or even a clear opposition regarding other goals between you and me. Trust, in the narrow sense defined here, can connect the players in an orchestra, a teacher and her student, a father and his son, but also a master and his slave, a conqueror and his captured enemy, or even a camp commander and his victims. Trust regarding an entrusted work or event can be accompanied by hostility, hatred, contempt, or abuse.

One could object that such relations are naturally accompanied by mutual distrust, while "entrusting" seems to suggest a more confidential relationship. However, even the cruelest master can burden a slave with a task, while trusting that the slave will accept and execute it, and the slave can choose not to revolt, but rather to trust that a good performance will prevent punishment. A second objection can then point out that the slave does not have a choice and consequently cannot "will" what the master wants or wills. However, the slave *can* choose to be punished, killed, or tortured instead of being left "in peace"—although, in most cases, the price for disobedience will be considered too high.[2]

Extreme cases, in which hardly any confidence is left between you and me, except a very thin, but still sturdy, relation of entrusting and "forced" achievement, are a warning not to restrict trust to cases of benevolent bonding, close camaraderie, or friendship. Even when trust develops into a form of mutual trusting between you and me, the presence of our bond and common purpose can still accompany a contentious, merely utilitarian or calculating relation. To what extent mutual trust normally would express, prepare, or follow from a friendly, confidential, amicable, or even loving relationship must be examined; but it is important not to range trust *a priori* among the good forms of human intersubjectivity, while seeing distrust as a bad kind of it. Many beings, among them quite a number of persons, deserve distrust from those who seriously try to be or to become good, whereas trust among murderers can be vicious. The idea that trust is a virtue must consequently be avoided.

WHO IS TRUSTWORTHY?

Often we use the words *trust* and *trustworthy* to characterize the overall character of a person. Some persons inspire confidence by their manner of speaking and listening, their prudent behavior, their emotional balance, and their humble presence. Especially when long-standing cooperation and shared experiences have made me acquainted with someone, I know whether this person can be trusted; if we have even become true friends, it is clear whether or not I should vouch for my friend. In all such cases *trustworthiness* is almost synonymous with "having a good character" or "being a good person"; and the right response is overall confidence. In this sense, trust is not one narrow aspect of certain relations, but rather the opposite extreme of a scale that connects the restricted aspect isolated above and the most encompassing form of trust.

With regard to the kind and the extent of knowledge that justifies our entrusting certain persons with specific tasks, we can safely state that we do not always need a scientifically guaranteed insight in their qualifications. Often, such knowledge is impossible, because too many conditions would be at stake. How has this candidate's work been done? How was her social demeanor, constancy, and general mood? Although we "count on" the persons who work with us, we do not use the word *trust* when we refuse to take any risk because we want to calculate or predict without fail what they in all circumstances will do. Unpredictable persons we do not easily trust, but all trust implies at least some uncertainty. Otherwise we would speak about calculation, proof, or deduction. In certain circumstances where we have no choice, we might even be forced to take a lot of risk. But in any case, strong evidence of frequently arbitrary behavior makes someone untrustworthy. Shouldn't we then also acquire some knowledge of the trustable person's past and future ways of willing? But how do I get acquainted with the habits of your will?

RISK AND FREEDOM

If I trust you, I presume that your behavior will show a certain degree of constancy and perseverance, which will not be interrupted by sudden changes of character or entirely unexpected manners. However, unless I have known you intimately for many years, I cannot predict exactly how you will behave if very dramatic events, such as a tsunami or a personal disaster, test your nerves. Moreover, even if you have gained my confidence, it is not impossible that you are in fact a smart swindler and an excellent actor or that you, after a period of reliability, have become corrupt.

Trust is not immune to disappointment and deception. It cannot rely on scientific demonstrations of someone's 100 percent trust-proof properties because this would exclude the trustee's freedom and such an exclusion is incompatible with the respect without which no trust can be sincere. Trusting you implies that, within the limits of our overall agreement or contrast, I leave it to you whether and how precisely you are and do what I trust you to be and do. Risk is therefore inherent in all trust. Calculating, using, checking all the steps and details of your performance would degrade you to an instrument or a thoroughly drilled animal. Counting on you stops being an aspect of my confidence as soon as I take you so completely for granted that I cannot even imagine how you could act against my expectations or that you, in unforeseen circumstances, would rightly decide not to accomplish what you had promised or agreed to do. Risk is therefore an integral element of trust—as essential and integral as the truster's recognition of the trusted person's being free and responsible for her own life and behavior.

Although liberty cannot be reduced to the arbitrariness of mere "choice," it cannot be disconnected either from the considerate and decisive responsibility of the actor's own decisions concerning her conduct. To trust someone includes the giving of credit. Trust, credit, risk, counting on, and reliability cannot be understood if we must choose between a conception of freedom that would define it as the capability of a completely unexpected and each time arbitrary choice from many possibilities or the idea that freedom can be so well-determined that it is bereft of all further initiative or self-revision.

HABITS

To understand how counting on the regular behavior of free persons does not contradict the incalculability of their actions, one might reread Aristotle's splendid analyses of habitual—virtuous or vicious—behavior.[3] Although free will plays an essential role in all human acting, this fact does not imply that each singular action, time and again, needs an entirely new deliberation and choice about the manner in which one should deal with the world, others, and oneself. Human freedom realizes itself primarily in the formation of a behavioral pattern that expresses—and thus characterizes—the orientation and motivation of the acting person. In the course of our praxis we develop particular and singular dispositions and patterns that show who and how we have become. Each of us is recognizable by a specific and singular manner of dealing, acting, living, and being. Because we have been free while practicing in a particular way, we have customary patterns and *habits* of *our own.* These habits give our behavior a certain continuity; together they form what we can call someone's *character:* the singular mode of each one's participation in human history. Each individual has a characteristic manner of moving, speaking, behaving, living. That is "typically Bush"; this is "vintage Obama," and so on. Each singular person's will has incarnated itself in habitual modes of acting and reacting, which together compose that person's observable unicity. *Character* resumes the characteristic manners that have become "normal" for the personalized existence of this or that individual in question.

Character, in this sense, does not exclude the possibility that a person, in exceptional circumstances, might display quite surprising behavior, but such exceptions would not amaze us, had we not become accustomed to the actor's usual way. I can count on you, you are trustworthy in my estimation, insofar as I, on the basis of my acquaintance with your past, reasonably may expect that you will fulfill certain tasks—for yourself, for both of us, and for others whom we care for. To be trustworthy, it is not enough that you have the required talents and skills; your "normal" behavior must also justify the expectation that you will not suddenly give up or disrupt the agreed upon or promised course of action. I trust that your characteristic way of solving problems guarantees satisfactory results and prevents uncharacteristic, arbitrary, or strange decisions that might derail a successful process.

The suspicion that trusting someone is impossible without implying some kind of determinism, is refuted by the fact that trust does not have to prescribe or check all the aspects or details of the task (work, behavior, life) that must be performed. On the contrary, by trusting you, I offer you an appropriate space for personal initiative and invention. The risk such liberality involves remains an essential ingredient of the trusting relationship. If this degenerates into the relation of a master who uses other individuals as will-less tools, the risk may be reduced to zero, but the quintessence of trust—respect for the other's selfhood—has vanished with it. Whether the master pays such tools does not make a difference: they remain slaves. Their situation is even worse than the situation of a *trusted* slave, because the denial of their own free willing reduces them to property, even if the pleasure this property provides, is "compensated" by money.

RECIPROCITY

Free will, initiative, and, to some extent, choice play a role in all that is typically human; they are essential not only in declaring that I trust someone, but also in accepting someone's offer that we enter into a mutual relation of trust. But what must we then call the relation of total dependence on the mother thanks to which a baby survives? Does the baby trust the mother—perhaps unconsciously? If we want to stretch the word *trust* to also characterize the behavior of babies with regard to their mothers, it does not seem easy to describe exactly what distinguishes such behavior from the spontaneity with which several kinds of very young animals cling to their parents; but the possibility of determining a stance of one's own grows with aging and therewith the degree in which a merely instinctive adhesion changes into a freely sought or accepted form of trust.

Trust can emerge unilaterally and mark one's life even when the trusted person is unaware of it. I can trust the religious authority or the literary taste of persons who died centuries ago; but mutual trust presupposes that you not only know, but also will—that is, want or accept—that I trust you *and* that you respond to my trust by trusting me. Such a response is not inevitable. To be trusted can be experienced as a burden, for if you trust me, I may be afraid that you will expect—perhaps even demand—too much from me. Don't exaggerate my capacity to help you with work or advice; you overestimate my competence; I do not have the time; I direct already too many dissertations, and so on. Or, thank you for your trust in me, but I cannot really trust you and I do not want to promise anything.

If you tell me that you trust me, I cannot avoid answering you, however. This fact is a specification of a general rule: as soon as someone addresses me by any word or gesture, I *must* respond (that is, I cannot avoid responding). Even falling silent or walking away is a response, and a clear, often rather insulting one. There is simply no way *not* to respond to a direct confrontation. But when you let me know that you trust me, the unavoidability of a response is a particularly urgent one, because your declaration not only reveals to me that you want me to engage in a special kind of relation, but also that you attribute certain qualities or powers to me, which—at least implicitly—you ask me to use, when needed, for your purpose(s). If I accept your trust in me, I thereby confirm at least the essence of your expectations, even if I might protest against certain aspects of your evaluation of my skills. Such a confirmation includes a promise: If and when I can, I indeed will help you. If I do not wish to promise anything, I should make this clear to prevent cruel disappointments; but it is not only difficult, it may also lack efficiency, to declare that I do not want your trust.

If my acceptance of your trust in me already implies a certain commitment on my side, which consequences follow then from a response in which I would answer your trusting me by an expression of my trusting you in turn? The mutual trust that emerges then seems to be part of a special kind of intersubjectivity. Such trust is normal in friendship and love, but it is also presupposed in contractual relations. The latter can lack all intimacy, but they do presuppose a personalized kind of tie, which cannot be completely reduced to a mere form of legal enforceability.[4]

That you trust me is by itself not a sufficient reason for me to trust you. Trust is not necessarily a virtue and my trusting someone does not make this person good. That you trust me certainly does not prove that I am indeed trustworthy, but only that you have found someone whom you deem trustworthy enough to put your confidence in. Trust in someone can accompany the other's and one's own perversions. Both trust and a particularized kind of trustworthiness function in criminal and immoral associations and socially or politically corrupt institutions. It remains true, however, that a declaration of being trustworthy ("Trust me!") implies a promise, although the declaration—and then also the promise—may be a lie. For what could such an encouragement mean, if the speaker does not have any intention to help or serve the audience?

Putting confidence in you, with the expectations implied in it, does not necessarily presuppose that you and I agree in all respects. It is sufficient that we agree on the particular nature and the quality of the performance that is expected from you, but your and my motivations for wishing the right result can be very different. You might, for example, have good reasons not to get involved in a farther-reaching plan or program that seems ideal to me but not to you. With regard to the limited task on which we agree, our motivations might be very different. Although we share a desire for a successful performance of the agreed work, our programs might be contradictory. In politics, such monstrous alliances are no exception.

EVALUATION AND DECISION

The establishing of a trust relationship between you and me presupposes at least the following conditions:

- In my judgment, you are competent to realize a goal that both you and I want to be realized (for example, your success in business or the well-being of my family or both).
- Your habitual demeanor justifies in my eyes the expectation of a successful outcome (you are a person who can promise).
- You have reasons for cooperating with me in the realization of the projected outcome and you trust that our cooperation will yield the desired effect; you therefore agree to contribute to the realization of the agreed goal.
- My evaluation of your capabilities and your evaluation of mine regarding the conditions of our cooperation justify both your

> and my judgment that, within the limits of our orientation toward the desired success, you and I are the right persons to here and now realize that success.

What still is missing among these conditions is the actual decision that you and I indeed decide to actually entrust one another with the common task that must be performed and the partial tasks that must be distributed among you and me. Indeed, it is possible not to decide thus, even if the four conditions listed above are realized. It is not always clear why, in these circumstances, I would decide not to ask you to realize the project. Perhaps I do not feel enough affinity with you or you are "not my type." But if entrusting you with a task for which you possess all the conditions does not automatically follow from my positive evaluation, then my decision to actually confide the task to you cannot be reduced to an evaluative judgment. And the same is true regarding your judgment about my role in the proposed cooperation The evaluation demands an additional element—we still must pass the threshold that marks, on one side of the decision, the difference between our knowledge of the particular talents and qualities that make you and me fit for the task and, on the other, the trusting relationship in which you and I decide to be effectively involved with one another's singular and unique personality. Neither your nor my personality can be summarized by the totality of its features or reduced to it. My confidence in you and your confidence in me is in the end not based on the composition of your or my properties but on your self and my self: these singular and irreplaceable, only-once-occurring selves, who cannot be replaced or equated with a combination of qualities, but, in their unicity, can only be recognized, approved, passed over, or effectively engaged.

By putting my trust in you, I confirm and honor you as irreplaceable, even if you can be replaced within the limits of your skills and professional properties. If you quit or die, I can limit my search to someone who fulfills all the "objective" conditions for a good performance, but then again the commitment we will make (or not) has its own irreducible decidability. Trusting someone thus involves more than a necessary or inevitable result of correct evaluations. There is always more at stake than a totality of properties, because trust or confidence is not the outcome of an evaluative calculation or the conclusion of an argument, but instead the decisive manner through which You and I, two unique and irreplaceable persons, confide and abandon a part of their own existence to an other unique person. In other words, trusting someone occurs always as an event that occurs in a strictly personal and interpersonal history, which thereby undergoes a change.

In connection with the distinction just made, it is useful to underline anew the difference between an objectifying and a "dative" approach. Trust cannot be characterized as a question of objective knowledge, although this may play a subordinate role in the judgment of the persons involved; but it is essential that they decide to unite their forces in a trusting and trusted form of common operation.

If, for example, a medical or psychological report reveals that a certain candidate is seriously ill, one will not entrust him with tasks that will be hindered by his illness. Objective knowledge is relevant, but the acquaintance that plays a preparatory role for the final decision cannot be *reduced* to an objectively true judgment or a correct evaluation. A more powerful motif is decisive. The qualities and past performance of the person who wins my confidence do not give her a right to my trust. Instead, she impresses me by a manner of dealing with people, things and projects that inclines me—but without forcing me—to risk a decision, through which I confide certain aspects of my well-being to her. My personal history, my desired but incalculable realization of my destiny is largely determined by the particular modes of my relating to particular persons who have accepted my trust in them as reason for intervening in my life.

INDEPENDENT AND FREE

By confiding in others with regard to plans that must be realized or events that should occur, I hand a part of my own concerns and tasks on to other free persons. Thus, I make myself dependent on the people whom I trust in exchange for a certain power over my life. At the same time I keep a certain form of initiative insofar as my trust, if sincerely accepted, ties the trusted ones to my own purpose(s). Moreover, I can withdraw my confidence, although I might have to pay a heavy price for it.

If I trust you, I do not force or blackmail you, because my trusting you testifies to your trustworthiness and freely chosen involvement by letting you perform in your own way. Both you and I respect each other's freedom, but we also limit it. Individual autarky is, in any case, not a good point of departure for acquiring insight into a relationship of trust. Even if the one whom I trust is not a friend or colleague, but instead an employee, he has his own initiative, rights of his own, and some degree of real power over me. He can go on strike, do things differently than I would like them to be done, or withdraw from the relation; but more detailed analyses must show how the interplay of freedom and dependence works out in different varieties of trust.

VERTICAL AND HORIZONTAL RELATIONS OF TRUST

For an accurate analysis of the dialectic of dependence and freedom within relationships of unilateral trust, it is useful, perhaps even necessary, to distinguish *hierarchical* or *vertical* relations, such as those between managers and employees, and *horizontal* relations between equals, such as colleagues, friends, parents, and children of one family.

Vertical relations of trust occur every day in many occasions and modes, for example, when we take a taxi or hire someone to paint the house. No one can indulge in the illusion that an isolated individual alone can fulfill all the conditions for his or her survival. Many people, who take care of such conditions, must be trusted, although I cannot prove that all of them will turn out to be trustworthy or will do their work well. We are never autarkic, but always dependent on others who, through their work or behavior, participate in our way of life. Trust is necessary where proofs, prophecies, and proven predictions are missing.

Accepting such dependence is hardly possible for people who equate freedom with unlimited choice or autonomy. They live in the illusion—a special kind of lie—that a human individual on his own can be the center of the world, capable of doing everything that is needed for living humanly. Individualists are good at talking about choice, autonomy, originality, and creativity, but what would remain of these marvelous attributes, if we could not count on the many mothers, nurses, educators, teachers, merchants, and so on, who must be trusted to make our survival and originality possible? Who would be alive and civilized if they did not take care of us? Perhaps we could have been saved by dogs or monkeys, but human culture would not be possible without human traditions, role models, and the teachers who train us in them.

Something similar is true of managers who entrust their subordinates with work. When the latter are emancipated, they might, in the name of their freedom, protest against the fact that they must listen to their bosses' instructions, but the bosses may answer that they likewise must give an account of their work to the superiors who have entrusted them with oversight. A thorough reflection on the concrete play of trust in various networks thus shows long, hierarchically ordered chains of trust and responsibility, which together encompass the entire society. By being players on appropriate levels, we keep traditions of cascading trust alive, which conditions the overall constellation of a trust-based social system.

Like speaking, the phenomenon of trust frustrates the question of who was the first person in time to trust someone else. Perhaps the question makes sense with regard to the idealized structure of a strictly monarchic community, because we then can ask: whose trust is primordial and ultimately responsible for the unity of the whole? But in fact, the beginning of all trust coincides with the first emergence of a human plurality—at least for trust in persons. Some individuals have tried to profile themselves as "the great leader" from whom all other functions and forms of subordinate entrusting spread out into terraces of subordinate leadership and execution. However, a supreme leader is not less dependent than the least powerful at the bottom of the social universe. As Plato's description of the tyrant makes abundantly clear, the man at the top, who deems himself the freest because he can choose whatever he wants, is in fact the slave of his slaves: more tied, addicted, chained, feared, hated, and imprisoned, but also less trusted, than all other members of the political community.[5]

ASYMMETRY AND EQUALITY

The preceding considerations suggest that the various relations in which trust becomes concrete encompass a large scale of gradations in dependence and autonomy. On each level of the social order, the participants are at the same time free *and* subordinate.[6] But can a trusted slave, in the name of his being trusted, still be called free? Insofar as a slave is not a thing or animal, but potentially even more civilized than his master, certainly. Epictetus, for example, clearly surpassed his master in wisdom and virtue. In these he equaled the Emperor Marcus Aurelius.[7] One way of being stronger than a threatening master or tyrant is, for example, telling him the truth about his arrogance or accepting death as a reward for one's own loyalty to truth and virtue. *A fortiori* the slave enjoys a high degree of autonomy, if the master has entrusted him with the education of his children.

In horizontal relations, the asymmetry between a master and his slave or between a director and her trusted assistant is replaced by the symmetry of mutual expectations on the same level. A friend trusts me like I trust her; we can count on one another. Such a symmetry entails neither that we are interested in calculating how many obligations and merits each one has toward the other, nor that we want to measure and compare the intensity of our feelings. If a friend asks me to do something, the request is not heard as a command, but she is confident that I will do whatever I can to accomplish her wish or, if that is impossible, that I will explain why her wish cannot be realized.

When a friend wants me to do something for her, she makes herself dependent on my cooperation, but at the same time she remains (co)responsible for my work and dedication. As friend, she does not refer to a higher level of entrusting that would justify her demands on me; our friendship must by itself be sufficient to make her confident that I will respond in an appropriate way. Friendship includes a point of departure—an origin and beginning—of its own, which is not derived from a hierarchy of social strata and the chains of obligations that come with them. Further analysis of the connections between trust and personal friendship on the one hand, and the social order, on the other, must clarify why trust between friends has a far greater independence with regard to economic and political networks than the trust that connects other members of such networks.

FUNCTIONING IN SOCIETY

Without trust we cannot function. A clarification of this fact can begin by remembering our own humanization. We would not have become human, if we had not confided, through an almost all-encompassing trust, in those who welcomed, nursed, trained, formed, and otherwise cared for us: parents, nurses, teachers, exemplary people, but also competitors, who themselves were formed by their instructors. This form of dependence has never stopped. However old we are, in order to continue participation in the ongoing histories to which we belong, we remain dependent on new information and updated learning. Maturity differs from childhood insofar as we have become more able and less dependent in our appropriation of the influences that mark our lives. Strictly individual experiences, selective reading, training, and studying are necessary but not sufficient for further progress toward wisdom and virtue; we continue to need trustworthy assistants and instructors. This need does not exclude that we utter critique or criticism, but even these presuppose that we continue to learn from past and present luminaries and traditions. Even all revolutions, such as the American, the French, the democratic, capitalist, and communist ones, have been inspired by timely retrievals of old incentives and forgotten or half-forgotten traditions.

Participation in the social and cultural history of our time depends not only on good advisers, up-to-date writers, and exemplary heroes, but also on the anonymous customs and shifting traditions of the culture in which we live. Contexts, tradition, ingrained mores, even revolutionary ideas and anonymous forces move our lives as elements of human history. Are they trustworthy? Can they be trusted as healthy, progressive, ennobling, and peace-loving factors?

In the mean time our meditation has made a transition from trust in persons to trust in collective trends and forces. Many assumptions, anonymous structures, rules, exigencies, and automatisms, examples of which can be found everywhere, capture our attention. We do not examine the chemical composition of bread before we eat it, but we trust that it is not poisoned. We do not use a lie detector when we ask someone where we can find the closest garage—although we might take some precautions in addressing our question to this or that person. Social mechanisms may be in or out of order, but in general we count on them being usable and trustable. We may have experienced how much a totalitarian system undermines the normal trust level of a peaceful society. To have lived under the Nazi occupation, for example, is a powerful antidote against an all too naïve eloquence about social and national trust. Bypassing or corrupting the judicial system, listening in on private conversations, stealing secrets, and organizing widespread suspicion are excellent means to instill distrust into the population. During the Bush-Cheney years we have seen how a nation that considers itself liberal is able to transform itself into an almost totalitarian organization. In countries where one sees more police than other persons populate the streets, while hearing too many stories about informants, distrust spreads to all persons and institutions, including even the privacy of cars, computers, homes (aren't they bugged?), and phones.

As individuals we cannot control the anonymous structures that dominate our world, but if we refuse to generally trust them, we had better move to deserts or untouched parts of nature. Even for participation in the savvy world of reporters, scholars, doctors, and psychiatrists, one needs a certain degree of suspicion, because no network seems immune against infiltration by pervasive powers. How could we feel safe and protected, when it is impossible to hold the disposition of all the other participants in check, especially when these enjoy much money or other powers? Aren't we too naïve in accepting the generally recognized results of the scholarly orthodoxy? When we realize that we can neither repeat the many experiences and experiments, nor rigorously check or recheck the plausibility of all the hypotheses on which that orthodoxy is based, we understand that its authority is conditioned not only by accurate observation, the best possible interpretation of documents, and excellence in logic, but also by our own trust in the work that has been done by physicists, psychologists, sociologist, and historians, among others.

Participation in the economic order and counting on the legal system—despite its inevitable deficiencies—would be impossible if we could not count on a minimal level of decency and trustworthy promises. Even more so, politics is first of all a question of trust and distrust. Hobbes's war of all the greedy and power-hungry wolves against all others who are as greedy, shows us how generalized egoism leads to universal distrust and how this changes politics into anarchic or organized murder and slavery. Once we discover—as we do daily—that such distrust is quite justified in many places on earth, we might wonder how it is possible that large populations still show at least some trust in their rulers and institutions.

Insofar as we, ourselves, are responsible for education, teaching, and producing cultural works or events, we owe our skills and a large part of our motivation to our trust toward the parents, educators, teachers, trainers, writers, researchers, and engineers who guide us, and, of course, to the moral, legal, literary, and religious traditions that have shaped and stylized us. This kind of trust can neither be abolished nor surpassed by self-made patterns of life. All independent or "autonomous" productions, however "original" they might be, are variations on patterns that, thanks to those authorities, were handed on. Even all forms of criticism, revolution, reform, and renaissance testify to a past that still deserves trust, although no past can be reproduced without transformation.

A bit of reflection about all these and similar levels of utter dependence-by-way-of-trust is sufficient to show how small the latitude is for individual choices and how ridiculous the words *autarky* or *independence* can sound.

Moreover, we have not yet even paid attention to the forces or powers that hide behind, underneath, and in all the dimensions of the cosmic and social universe into which we, without any chance of choice, have come to live. Is trust an appropriate answer to the question of whether this unchosen but occurring universe, with its ongoing history of splendor and horror, has a meaning? What does human existence mean? And what should we trust or distrust of the recurring myths that we find everywhere about gods and demons, fate and destiny, "God" and God?

TWO

Entrusting

Several authors have analyzed the interpersonal relation that emerges when someone entrusts someone else with a message, a mission, the conservation of some property, an intelligent contribution to a debate, and so on. Before focusing in more detail on the phenomenon of entrusting someone with a certain task, I summarize here a few relevant points that have already been noted in chapter 1.

The trusting person trusts that the trusted person is (a) competent and (b) willing to (c) do (accomplish, produce, speak) what the trusting person asks, expects, or hopes to be done, although there is always a certain risk that cannot be eliminated by any calculation or deduction.

By trusting someone, I do not supply the missing link for a demonstration of the fact that the trusted one certainly *will* realize what I trust her to do. With someone whom I trust, I deal differently than I would deal with a person whose behavior I want to study and comprehend (or even calculate) so well that I can predict without fail the result of her doing with regard to the thing or the task I entrust to her. By putting my trust in you ("I trust you"), I situate myself in relation to you, while stating, deciding, or affirming—at least implicitly—that you, according to me, are trustworthy. Which people are trustworthy? Persons of whom I have sufficient experience to expect that they *will* accomplish what I trust them to do, although they might—perhaps, "God forbid"—disappoint my expectation and estimate of its probable fulfillment.

It is not necessary that the trusted person know about my trusting her, but it is essential that she not be forced to do what I want her to do; she must do it out of her own responsibility. While turning to you, whom I trust, I ask you to do (be, omit, and so on) what—I trust—you can and, once you accept my request, will do. I delegate a task—either one that I could accomplish on my own or one for which you, rather than I, are competent, but in any case I count on you to perform it in your way, taking your own responsibility for it. In a sense, I leave you alone with that task, which, as yours, is somehow an extension or replacement of my own task. You have become an extension of me and I am with you as long as you are working on the task. By putting my trust in you, I accompany you, even if neither you nor I are constantly aware of it. Parts of your and my life and responsibility coincide by participating differently in one and the same work. My trust in you can be motivated (at least in part) by recommendations I have received, but in the end, it is my estimate and my decision—which involves a certain risk—on which my trust depends.

Trusting someone can be a one-sided relation, which does not necessarily trigger an equivalent trust in the trusted person. For example, when I trust that a particular student will become a great scholar, my telling her neither generates automatically her trust in me, nor does it necessarily trigger any self-confidence in the student. My trust in someone can even be answered by contempt, for example when the trustee is not impressed by my discernment or when he has faked his trustworthiness to mislead the trusting one.

Many variations are possible and the summary structure sketched above can be applied and modified in relation to trust in things, tools, property, one's own mental and corporeal capacities, social institutions, language, culture, mores, humanity, the world, the universe, being, and God, but one important distinction between *trusting* and many other human activities must be stressed, because it is often overlooked. To clarify this distinction, I begin with another distinction which I already mentioned in chapter 1: the distinction between *speaking to* and *speaking about.*

SPEAKING ABOUT AND SPEAKING TO

When I *speak about* something, I place myself at a certain mental distance from that thing, as it is there displayed in front of me. I can also speak about persons, of course, for example by giving information about their function, their qualities, work, successes, and so on. This kind of speaking keeps them at a distance; it does not create a bond between me and the person about whom I am speaking. *Speaking to,* however, does: by addressing you, I turn to you by approaching, facing, confronting, affronting, and engaging you in a personal relation, which bridges the distance between you and me. If you respond to my addressing you by addressing me, our association is a fact. Such an association can be broken off: the bridge can be forgotten or destroyed; my speaking *to* you *can* be followed by only speaking to others *about* you, but my speaking to you does not change you into an *object* for me.

Scientists and philosophers are spontaneously inclined to observe, thematize, objectify, and think *about* the subject matter, theme, or object of their scholarly interest. Since, today, almost everything that happens or draws interest, is shown on screens and endlessly displayed in presentations and representations, the displaying and (re)presentational mode of showing, observing, and thinking has become one of the most overwhelming modes of dealing with things and gadgets, tools, clothes, homes, landscapes, art works, events, movements, and persons, and even with feelings, desires, and thoughts. We are obsessed with seeing, picturing, and putting things before our corporeal and mental eyes. Looking at TV is paradigmatic here for our perspective on the world in which we live, especially when we are trained in science or philosophy.

Most of us have a strong tendency to approach the reality as *being there:* as waiting for us in order to be exhibited, mastered, studied or thematized from a freestanding viewpoint without other commitment than that of an unlimited curiosity. To view and overview, to draw maps and enjoy panoramas, to display and observe from a distance, or—in general—to *objectify* has become the preferred way of perception, especially in scholarship. But are we aware of the impoverishment that is caused when this type of relation (or "intentionality") becomes a monopoly? Fortunately, at least one other relation cannot be abolished: a mode of dealing with reality that does not allow itself to be reduced by objectification.

This other relation imposes itself on anyone who approaches or encounters someone else by greeting, gesturing, turning, and speaking to that person, who, by such modes of contact, neither is, nor can be changed into, a displayable object. An object can be known by looking at it from all its sides, and I can speak *about* it at length without being involved in it. Speaking *to* someone however—for example, in the form of a greeting ("Hello!")—cannot be reduced to any "content" or "message" that thereby is delivered. If such speaking also contains a message that can be objectified, displayed, or thematized in a scholarly way (but what is the message or "content" of "Hello" or "Hi!"?), this "content" does not cover the addressing act by which it is carried, targeted, and transmitted. The transmitting of anything we say (something that is said or "the said" conveyed by a saying)—the *speaking to* or *addressing* as such—does not coincide with any "proposition" in the current sense of analytic epistemology or linguistic philosophy. However, it *is* an active, oriented, and directed proposing (or proposal), insofar as it brings the speaker's speaking to the fore in order to make contact with the one who is addressed, confronted, faced. In chapter 1, we introduced the very fundamental distinction between speaking to and speaking about (or between addressing and message), and we will return to it. First, however, let us pursue the general question of how trust relates to that distinction.

Trust is not an objectifying attitude, act, or activity, but rather a simultaneously receptive and active turning toward someone else that associates me with the trusted one, while encouraging the latter to take responsibility for the entrusted task. Trusting someone belongs to the family of relations that connect one person with one or more others in the mode of attention, targeting, addressing, doing something to, letting go, and expecting something from them. This class of relationships has hardly been studied in the philosophical literature, despite their basic relevance for all human communication. As long as our thinking about phenomena cannot free itself from its drive to an all-encompassing objectification, we remain guilty of scholarly ignorance with regard to the most basic relations of human interaction, dialogue, and conversation, with which even children are acquainted, because *they form and maintain the core of all sociality.*

Trust is one of the basic connections that cannot be captured as relations between an observing, displaying, thematizing, objectifying *subject* and an observed, displayed, thematized *object.* The relation that links a subject to an object is neither universal, nor adequate for characterizing interpersonal and social relations. When a subject sees or treats another as an object, the latter is reduced to features that can be perceived, displayed, described, used, and dominated, whereas looking, listening, or speaking to the other prevents such objectification by permitting the other subject to come forward as another center of the world. Objectification leads to subordination or absorption. The second subject is then in danger of becoming an appendix to the primary subject, which most often is identified as (an) I, and this I sees itself then as a transcendental I, who either looks down on each object-I or absorbs it as a moment of its own, egoic experience and adventure. Only if we can free the "subject" or "me" from its objectifying perspective—so that it becomes or remains open to the greatest possible variety of relations, many of which escape Ego's panoramic perspective—can we remain faithful to the interpersonal facts as we experience them in the performance of human existence.

In trust, and in many other ways of approaching others, we are engaged in a *turning to* them, as chapter 1 explains. With regard to the objectifying mode of our scientific profession, this turn demands a difficult conversion. We must become again a wholly receptive openness in face of the other who addresses us, if we want to discover who, how, and what this other subject offers from out of her own ek-sisting. By confronting me, the other puts me into a position that either welcomes her or shuts the door. I have to adopt an attitude that responds to the confrontation instead of changing the other's frontal address into the givenness of an object. Persistence in scientific "objectivity" would reduce the encounter to a phenomenon in which none of the confronted subjects personally encounters the other. Are we, as researchers, forced to reduce each and every topic to an object, while maintaining ourselves outside the drama, which we anyway are performing? In that case, in science or philosophy we would remain uninvolved, neutral subjects without intersubjective contacts. But would such a duality not split us into double subjects? If, however, we turn away from objectification, would that not exile us from all serious concentration on displayable things and persons? Must thinking in science or philosophy necessarily be limited to a thinking *about* things—and about persons, as if they were mere objects? Are we, as researchers, obliged to reduce each and every topic to an object, while maintaining ourselves as onlooking and uninvolved subjects?

The answer is no, at least if *thinking* is understood as a name for the whole of philosophy or any other science. For what would our discoveries, analyses, lessons, and writings mean, if they were not made available and conveyed by speaking *to* students, writing *for* readers, borrowing *from* and communicating *with* colleagues? Nothing of all possible knowledge would even exist for us, if we had not been educated, taught, introduced into civilization, language, culture, science, and philosophy by others who spoke to us because they trusted that we could learn from them. We listened to them because we trusted that they knew what they said. The information they provide would not exist for them either, if they had not received most of what they know from trustworthy others—and so on. Speaking, writing, communication, teaching, progress, transformation, the entire history of civilization rely on an endless procreation of trustworthy and trusting persons, who know how to explain and transmit the available texts, tools, and practices to the heirs of their heritage. If any of the components that are essential for civilization is missing—and among them, the innumerable instances of a trusting that does not (or not yet or never will) coincide with rigorous demonstrations—we will be miserable animals as long as our desire to establish the social, technical, amicable, and other conditions for knowledge and good practice does not die.

TOWARD AN ETHICS OF TRUST

By being aware of our connections with other researchers from whom we can learn, while being eager to discover together more about trust than we already know, we trust a whole range of assumptions whose reliability we have never demonstrated. We are turned to one another by welcoming and expecting, speaking, and listening. We are confident of not being in murderous company; we trust the various competences of our colleagues, and, although we know or may presume that many human and professional differences divide us, we are quite confident that our exchange is useful and probably will yield some positive result. The event in which we are involved when we discuss a common topic, illustrates that trust cannot be avoided. It would of course be possible to study the CVs, publications, manuscripts, and handouts of all our colleagues, but even an all-encompassing examination of their credentials, especially in fields outside of each one's own specialty, would not exclude all ignorance and risks from our meeting. Apparently we have other ways of measuring the trustworthiness of our colleagues and getting involved with them as serious interlocutors. Trust thus is unavoidable, but can we distinguish good and bad forms of trust? In other words, do we need an ethics of trust?

Elsewhere I have proposed to accept appropriateness as the basic standard for a philosophical ethics.[1] The words *appropriate* and *ethical* must then be understood in a broad sense. Allow me to sketch briefly how such a standard can be clarified and concretized with regard to genuine forms of trust.

In our encounters with persons, events, things, and other phenomena, including the world, humanity, and the universe, we are addressed and affected by what we are not. Affection is experienced as some change within my own corporeal and mental existence. It is felt, and once I feel affected, the particular affection, as uniquely singularized in me (you do not feel my affection), depends not only on the particular quality of the affecting reality, but also on many properties that characterize me, the individual person, who has to adjust to the affecting reality. I mention here only two aspects of this affection:

> The affection by which I am affected summons a *response;* it draws my attention toward the affecting reality, which, through its affecting, challenges me to react.
>
> The particular and individual character of the affecting phenomenon suggests a particular and personal—and thus unique—kind of answer and this suggestion guides my attempt to come up with an *appropriate* response.

On the basis of these assumptions, while trying to reconcile some basic elements of the Platonic-Aristotelian tradition with the relevance of Levinas's phenomenology of the face, which I take to be paradigmatic for the suggestive force of *all* phenomena, I trust that the following outline of ethics can be defended.[2]

Facing as your facing-me invites and summons me to *be for* you by adopting a well-adjusted attitude in your favor. Extending the relationship of your facing-me to other phenomena—such as paintings, songs, dogs, flowers, trees, mountains—we may state that I am faced and affected by a multilayered world of challenges, each of which evokes in me an appropriate mode of responding according to the summons of its phenomenal singularity. All particular phenomena incorporate, in various degrees of urgency, a proper and analogous mode of summoning and triggering human responses. Since the affected person is free (that is, living a life in which an individual self is seeking and probing its own way of experimenting and deciding), the factual responses cannot be predicted, but they can be evaluated: are they indeed appropriate?

When we apply these generalities to questions about trust, we can start from the simple statement—almost a tautology—that only *trustworthy* people deserve to be trusted. But who is trustworthy?

One condition for being considered to be trustworthy is to be competent in performing the specific and singular task that is entrusted. Such competence depends on the particular skills that are needed for accomplishing the entrusted activity. Depending on the work I would like to see accomplished, I am looking for a good contractor, a surgeon, a smith, or a security officer. If I look for someone to whom I can confide my children for a good education, I hope to find someone who has skills, tastes, ideas, and ideals of which I approve. If the dimension at stake is clearly moral, I cannot entrust my own or others' formation to guides who lack decency, genuineness, good manners, or exemplary behavior. On the political level I will not trust hypocritical politicians who, in fact, do not care for the common good. Among philosophers I want to be as sure as possible of their excellence; and in religious questions I am looking for someone who dislikes superstition and false pathos. An ethics of trust can focus on many varieties of human competence in order to find out how they affect their own and others' lives and what kind of trust they deserve.

When I ask a young philosopher to do research on Levinas's early essays, for example, I trust that her results will be useful, because she has already shown (either to me or to colleagues whom I trust) that she understands other works of Levinas. My trust is motivated by her demonstrated competence. I cannot predict or prove that further results will be as good as I hope for, but the risk is small and I am not really afraid that I err in counting on a good result.

The entrusted task must often be performed for the benefit of the entrusting person or institution. Once accepted, one performs what the truster wants to be done. The performance is then willed by both parties, but a major part of it is realized by the one who has accepted the execution of the project. One could even say that the latter realizes a part or an aspect of the productive *life* that the truster wants to realize. By entrusting a part or aspect of my ongoing life to someone else, the latter's work (a part of her life) coincides with a part of my—the truster's—projected life, which, in this case, is not being realized by myself but by the other. Two lives have become partially united; we share an embryonic form of common life, although our contributions are different. Is this not an aspect of all social life?

Trust does not only imply that the truster and the trusted focus on the same project. Besides competence in performance, a *second* essential condition is that both parties are *freely* willing the realization of the work at stake. If I force someone to do something for me, this does not express my trust in her, although I might trust her skills. Force or constraint reduces the other person to an instrument, a machine, or a will-less property. I then pursue the realization of my plan by means of threats, drill, or blackmail, but not by trust in her own responsibility. The other's work could eventually be done by a sophisticated robot. Trusting someone, for example a nurse, implies that I respect and positively support her own dedication as the source of her work for me (and this "for me" can be altruist; it can, for instance, consist in someone's being a "doctor without borders"). The trusted person's will must be confirmed by gratefully willing it as the other's responsible acceptance of my request that she realize a component of my life, while realizing also, and primarily, her own.

As mentioned in chapter 1, entrusting unites the persons involved by bringing them together in the realization of a common purpose, but the motivations and activities of the parties can differ considerably. Insofar as your and my will target the same result, our wills coincide, but your decision to accept my request might be motivated by something very different than mine, for instance not by the conditions of my job, but by an honorarium, friendship with me, interest in the project, or by a mixture of motivations, some of which may be more noble than others. From trusting in the terms of a contract that promises payment, to pure benevolence, many interests can move the other's activity, but in all cases there is an expectation—and to this extent also an (explicit or implicit) promise: the truster will be satisfied or dissatisfied, moved to acceptance, gratitude, reward, and praise, or—if the performance lacks the required quality—to protest and lack of appreciation. Because it is essential for the trust relation that the trusted person's purpose be willed by the truster, and vice versa, that purpose (though often seen and wanted from different perspectives) is a part of both lives involved. The respect that is implied in trust thus combines honoring the other's independence with agreement on the work to be done. Despite differences in activity and motivation, the performance of the work thus testifies to an aspectual (or partial) identity of two wills.

By making my project dependent on your performance, I recognize that I am not able or do not want to do myself what you can and want to do. To confide in you for a desired realization shows not only how much I esteem your competence; it also shows my profound respect for the free originality of your behavior. If you answer my request by accepting it, I cannot consider such acceptance—and your consequent activity—to be the effect of any performance of my own. That you indeed do what I ask you to do is never a conquest or acquisition, comparable to any acquisition of property. Your acceptance is always a gift, which naturally causes gratitude. (And gratitude can never be bought or annulled by money).

Discovering someone's competence never creates an obligation to confide in that person or entrust her with some work. The true worth of good skills must be recognized, but trust presupposes that the skillful person freely offers or accepts to use them, while urging the entrusting person to trust her as able and willing to perform the desired work. The willingness expressed in such an offer contains a *lesson* (you need me) and a *promise* (I will realize what you will), but also a hint of *union.* Indeed, the wills involved in a trusting relation are one insofar as they target a common part or aspect of two lives. When trust plays on a basic, central, or sublime level of human existence, and especially when the trust is mutual, the commonly willed and shared reality—for example guidance in moral or religious progress—covers much more than just a fragment of both lives in question. An old definition of friendship explains it as "willing and unwilling the same." Willing what you will, hating what you hate, isn't this an aspect of love? If trust unites two wills in the realization of a project, does it then realize a seed of love? In any case, it seems to bring people together and unite them through a peaceful agreement about working and willing. Perhaps it even realizes a beginning of love by uniting different persons without violence—at least temporarily and in some respect. Can union-in-trust become total among humans? Death and suffering seem to warn us that, "in the end," each of us lives alone. "Friendship until death"? Or is it possible that human wills reach beyond death—and thus might realize an undivided union of wills and lives that resists definitive isolation?

ENTRUSTING OR ACCEPTING?

The type of trust that we have analyzed emphasizes the wills of the persons involved: the will of a person who takes the initiative for an activity that the other, to whom this activity is entrusted, is willing to perform. By performing the task, the latter affects the former, which affection conditions and summons the former to respond; for example, by obligating him to pay the contracted price for the work done or by expecting some sign of contentment or gratitude. Having done what I asked you to do, you will expect that I will fulfill the explicit or implicit promise that lay in my request: you naturally trust that I recompense or thank and recommend you in turn.

The simple model of interpersonal trust just sketched can be extended and modified by varying the number and the qualifications of persons, by replacing persons with institutions, or by complicating the purposes and plans that must be realized. For example, I can ask a team of scholars to participate in a project that I inaugurate or direct; we might trust—or distrust—the support of a community, a nation, a church, or an alliance for a crusade against poverty. We trust entire networks that condition our communication. We trust the regularities of nature, but distrust the season of hurricanes, which prompts us to build dams and dikes. According to my personal experiences, I may trust or partially distrust my own health, my diet, the rhythms and capabilities of my body, the working of my heart and my brain, the given and acquired skills of my mind, my use of language, my taste for music and poetry, and so on. In these latter examples, however, it is not primarily my will that entrusts these forces with the realization of my plans. The initiative rather comes from the forces that allow me to use and count on their regularities for support of what I—thanks to their "willingness"—wish to be realized. Am I the one who entrusts them with their performance? Is it not rather they that tolerate my will's insertion into their course of action? What sort of "will" could we ascribe to them? True, several of those anonymous forces—human-made machines, communication systems, windmills, and dikes—are products of human will and intelligence, and this is even more obvious for cultural and historical aspects of life, such as the style of an epoch or a nation's language and moral code. But the structure of my trust in them, made possible by their allowing me to fit into their well-established dominance, shows that it is not me, but rather their power that conditions my submission to their manners of effective operation. Must I ascribe some kind of command or will to these powers? With regard to our trusting them (and the accompanying part of fear that they might betray this trust)—and, in general, with regard to our dependence on nature and culture—we may ask whether those powerful conditions are animated by some dispensation, a superhuman *psyche* or spirit perhaps, a fate or destiny that decides about our possibilities in a more or less trustable, hopefully prosperous, but sometimes trying or cruel manner. Whatever the answer is, our experiences of trust and distrust (accompanied by fear and hope—and gratitude) force us to reconsider a human motto that, since Descartes, has been celebrated in Western civilization: the motto of making ourselves "masters and possessors of nature"[3]—to which we, as children of a technological era, may be tempted to add: "masters of human civilization and history."

Masters and manipulators of nature, culture, and history. Has this motto finally died—not only in popular culture but also among intellectuals and philosophers? Have nature itself and history revindicated their part of indomitable sovereignty, forcing humanity to mourn its periodic phantasies about conquering and owning its own destiny by transforming it into a *will to Will*? Or is "the Will" a metaphor for that which remains a humanly unwillable, but hopefully reliable Power on which civilization and history ultimately depend?

Starting from an individual will that urges another's will to responsibly join the former in executing (part of) a determinately willed task, we are also confronted by phenomena that resist an explanation of trust as entirely dependent on the willingness of human individuals who join their wills in mutual confidence. What about trust in the anonymous powers that condition our survival and successes, while accompanied by fear that they might disappoint us and put us in a more humble place or destroy us entirely? Again and again, our fate is decided by a singular combination of fortune or misfortune and personal or collective adjustments to it. A stoic response is radically different from cynical or triumphant ones, but in all cases utter dependence is the core of all variations. From trust in computers and markets to trust in the course of history, trust refers to powers or *wills* that cannot be possessed as private or public property. They must be accepted, perhaps even venerated, as all too mighty, but it seems also possible to befriend them as more trustworthy than terrifying blows of fate.

PART II: What and Whom Can We Trust?

The first part of the present book focused on trust between individual persons, and especially on one person, often indicated by the pronouns *I* and *me,* who trusts another person, supposed to be trustworthy. The simplicity of this model was defended by the remark that more complicated trust relations can be interpreted as modifications of its formal structure.

Instead of analyzing trust in one person, one can examine the differences that emerge when this person is replaced with a multiplicity of persons, or with communities, several kinds of institutions, animals, natural elements, frameworks, historical phenomena, and so on.

It is also possible to change the relation on the side of the trusting term, for example, by studying how an audience, a multiplicity of critics, an army, or a national majority reacts to trustworthy or untrustworthy personalities or decisions.

A third direction for modification is given by the possibility of specifying the entrusted work or the conditions of its realization.

In part 3, I will maintain the central position of the trusting persons under the names *he, she,* or *I* (the latter of which facilitates avoidance of gendered language); except that *we* and *they* or *us* and *them* will also be used when more individuals than one are meant. I will not investigate whether or how trusting is or can be done by nonhuman subjects or by some collective entity that cannot be reduced to a multiplicity of individuals, such as a nation, an alliance, an epoch, or the whole of humanity.

Of those realities that can be trusted or distrusted (for example, with regard to the "entrusted" tasks or processes they are supposed to perform), only three rather unspecified candidates will be highlighted in the following short chapters:

(1) In what sense and to which extent can (or must) I (or we) trust (or distrust) the *society* in which we live? (chapter 3)

(2) Can I trust or distrust the natural universe of which I am a part? (chapter 4)

(3) Can I trust or distrust myself? If so, in which sense am I then at the same time identical with or different from myself? (chapter 5)

Both nature and society are collective realities and more external to the trusting subject (me) than the subject itself, which maintains its central perspective in this book. The reflexive relation that characterizes self-confidence contrasts my relation to myself with my relation to the universe of society and nature (including their histories), while, at the same time keeping myself involved in that universe. The entanglement of relations that then comes to the fore prepares the main question of part 3: What or whom is the most trustworthy: the universe, I myself, the union of myself and the universe, or still another reality?

None of these chapters claims to give an exhaustive treatment of the indicated topics; but some of the aspects that are not emphasized in this part will be considered in chapter 8, where they figure as components of the universe.

THREE

Trust in the Society

Before and immediately after our birth we are not yet able willfully to trust or distrust anyone or anything, because both attitudes presuppose a minimum of liberty. However, if we can say of some dogs, rabbits, birds, horses, cows, and camels that they trust their masters, we may use the words *trust* and *distrust* also in some prevoluntary sense of babies. In any case, the early education we underwent without choosing it taught us whom to trust and whom not to trust. Over the years, we discovered that no human individual can survive without relations to trustworthy persons and institutions and how dangerous it is to be surrounded by individuals who deserve more distrust than trust. Discernment of trustworthiness is indeed one of the most important social skills for being successful in living a human life—almost as important as being perceived and approached as trustworthy and trust-inspiring oneself. Both must therefore be learned in order to become a well-functioning member of the society to which one belongs.

WHOM CAN I TRUST?

Since we are not just members of humanity, but also members of a particular family, inhabitants of a particular village or town, a nation with a specific culture, a particular language group, and, perhaps, a church or religion, our socialization implies diversification. This presupposes that each individual identifies with a particular language, particular customs and affinities, and a particular style of life. The particularity of the group to which we belong, our fitting within the limits of a specific community,[1] allows for a certain degree of mutual trust within that community, but it also creates a certain distance—which may cause distrust—with regard to those who are perceived as dissimilar to our own type of life. Within our own family, tribe, or class, trusting others is much easier, but even there, each one's singular individuality may cause tension and distrust or a delay of trust.

While growing up, we spontaneously trusted our parents and early educators, who constantly showed their care for our survival and development, but we also were frightened when terrifying events elicited anxiety or suspicion. Further acculturation has set our personal patterns and standards for trustworthiness and its contrary. We have learned to look at the eyes of interlocutors and to listen to the intonation of their voices in order to wager on their sincerity and benevolence or to detect their lies and hypocrisy. Does this person indeed perform what he seems to promise? Is she really interested in me and my interests? And so on.

Because we owe our first humanization to those who were close to us, trust in others will normally have made a stronger impact on us than occasions that inspired distrust. Further experiences have confirmed our impression that, in general, the advantages of association with others justify a basic sort of cautious trust, although one cannot disregard its interruption by nasty events that trigger distrust. Consequently, an individual's socialization includes the emergence of a personal balance of trust and distrust. This balance is a feature of each individual's character, but it may change over time because of the turns and twists that shake our existential adventures. Some individuals will turn out to be rather naïve in trusting too quickly or too much, whereas others, more anxious, indulge in exaggerated forms of suspicion.

It seems impossible to draw a picture of the ideal balance of trust and distrust, because much depends on the persons one meets and the circumstances in which these encounters take place. The quality of the existing order or disorder that determines the climate of a common space plays an especially weighty role. We cannot talk about trust in abstraction from the trustworthiness of the society in which the involved parties meet. The question of individual trust is linked to the other individuals' trustworthiness and this question implies the question of our society's mendacity or sincerity. For, it is indeed impossible to separate completely my trusting or distrusting you from the general degree of trustworthiness that characterizes our community, business, friendship, or collegiality. At the same time, however, we must distinguish the two questions because one may be trustworthy despite the generally accepted mendacity of a certain milieu.

CAN WE TRUST OUR SOCIETY?

In the previous chapter, we focused on the appropriate skills and the willingness of a person to whom I want to entrust a limited task. Someone deserves trust, who is not only capable of accomplishing a specific work, but also willing to accomplish it according to the conditions set for it (within the agreed time, for example). Motivation and scope are here tied to a limited operation that, once fulfilled, annuls the special relation between the persons involved. The time of trust is then limited by the conditions of the entrusted reality. If this reality encompasses more than a single operation, the compass and character of the trust that links the involved persons changes. With regard to a business partnership or a team-taught course, much information and assurance is needed about my colleague. Trust among intimate friends, spouses, or family members stretches its horizon beyond the limits of particular tasks to be accomplished; and to a certain degree this is also true of all other kinds of communities: township, state, nation, continent, or humanity. The trust we need when traveling, for example, has a diffuse and general character, which does not need specification, because ideally it covers all needs of all other members of the human society. Mutual trust about everything is here the ideal limit.

A truly all-encompassing trust in someone else would equal the entrusting of my own *life* to that person. But such would be possible only if I could abandon the entirety of my existence (including all my actions and experiences) to someone who would be knowledgeable and powerful enough to take care of my life without taking away my own responsibility for it. The reliance of infants on their parents could be seen as symbolic for the unfree part of such an all-encompassing trust. But is a total abandonment to others' unlimited capability and benevolence, while at the same time freely performing one's own existence, possible? The idea of my entrusting all the details of my own adult life to an all-encompassing *human*—communitarian or historical—trustworthiness cannot coexist with my own freedom, because I should not and cannot abolish the moment of initiative that constitutes my individual humanity.[2] However, all of us entrust much of our behavior and knowledge to the various communities to which we belong; and we belong to them not by a completely unconditioned choice but rather by acquiescence, acceptance, consent, and appropriation. Indeed, the family into which we are born, the ethos and the language of our nation, the culture and the religion in which we happen to be educated marked us before we were asked whether we wanted or even could trust them. When we are asked this question today, the only honest answer is that a quite particular combination of language, culture, belief, and so on continues in each of us on the basis of a hardly self-conscious or self-willed mode of general trust, although we might once in a while be irritated by some doubts. We are and remain products of the particular societies (family, nation, church, friendships, and other associations) that have formed us according to their particular function and character. Our general trust is the imprint we have received from those societies that, through their culture and subcultures, "made" us what and how we are (like "England made me," for example). Of course, our freedom plays a role in the integration of that legacy into the personal performance of our destiny, but even our doubts and critical responses to the acculturation we underwent are only variations or—if they are important—transformations of the heritage we received. We could not even trust ourselves (and our criticisms) at all, if we were not supported by a basic trust in the legacies we received from the various communities that helped us to mature.[3]

If we owe gratitude to our parents and educators for having made our growth and development possible, we owe part of it to the cultural traditions and institutions of our nation that made our humanization possible. Insofar as family and school conditioned our development, our parents must be praised for having entrusted parts of our education to institutions that transmitted the dominant ethos and culture to us. In corrupt and criminal nations, homeschooling might be the only decent way, but even some decadent or horribly totalitarian states might deserve a small amount of trust to the extent to which they save their children from becoming barbarians or inveterate criminals. Insofar as a society itself is barbaric, violent, or unjust, one should neither trust nor collaborate with its purposes and decisions, but the totalitarian systems of the twentieth century have shown most dramatically how difficult it is to avoid impure compromises between public corruption and private decency. The entanglement in a rotten situation results in many tainted characters, but fortunately also in a considerable number of exceptional heroes. Generic distrust is certainly a recommendable response to such a situation. Even there trust might still find a few hidden dimensions where decency is possible; but who can find comrades decent and unafraid enough to accept bitter suffering for sharing dissidence? Even in nations where public institutions seem to foster honesty, one is not quite free from having dirty hands. Is the entire world not dominated by the blatant injustice of an economic and financial system in which everybody is caught? Who, for example, can be innocent and survive while participating in a system that makes the poor poorer while making the ultrawealthy wealthier? Or, to give another example of unavoidable negotiation and compromise, the so-called free world permits "free speech" within certain limits that seem free enough to many of its inhabitants, but unofficial and official voices are quick to accuse the critics of unpatriotic or disloyal speech. Not all critics preach total distrust or revolution in the name of some utopian ideal, however; and those who do, discover quickly that no revolution is possible without maintenance of some tainted elements of the law and order they want to overturn. Even a total overhaul needs trust—not only in the assurance of the reformers but also in more or less acceptable remainders of a ruinous past.

TRUSTWORTHY CONSTITUTIONS?

The question of trust regarding public institutions has been debated for thousands of years. From the perspective of trust versus distrust, it is very difficult to decide which is the best and the most trustworthy of the many models that have been tried out or proposed. History has shown that identical models can be managed in decent but also in horrendous ways, according to the mentality of the users. Legal constitutions cannot fully guarantee their actual concretization in the historical reality of a shifting population; loopholes are exploited by the parasites; some nations that call themselves democratic are in fact oligarchies of unelected banks, concerns, and lobbyists, while the modern monarchies of Europe are much more democratic than such so-called democracies. The president of the United States has considerably more powers than the queen of England or the king of Spain, whereas the labor unions of the Netherlands enjoy more rights and socio-political influence than the American ones.

To know whether one can trust the national society of which we, through birth or immigration, have become members, it is not sufficient to know the constitution of the country, because legal structures are too abstract to be trusted if they are not confirmed by an effective course of actions, periodic reinforcements and adaptations, events, and decisions that make people feel themselves recognized and more than tolerated: respected as participants and players in one common life-concerned process.

In every epoch of world history, some intelligent yet unhappy people have not only criticized the historical societies in which they had to participate, but also expressed their desire for radical reform by writing drafts of what they considered ideal constitutions. Not all of them realized that their utopias borrowed many of their features from the existing society, which soon would be outdated anyway, and that in politics it is not possible to begin from scratch, because the existing society cannot be wholly overturned, but only changed more or less thoroughly. This means that much of what is already in place, must survive, however regrettable this may be. The twentieth century has given us dreadful examples of utopian violence in Germany, Russia, China, and Cambodia—and the story goes on. Conservative spirits may use these examples as arguments against revolution, on the condition that they themselves admit that their own society, as heritage of the past, needs constant change to keep pace with the inexorable course of world history. Indeed, to be trusted, a society should not only be well organized and well run for the present but also be able to satisfactorily change over time—especially when one observes already symptoms of its decadence.

Can we trust a society whose "spirit" or mentality is very different from our own? With "spirit" I mean the inspiration of its *ethos,* as expressed in its dominant manners and *mores.* Can I recognize my own affective, moral, and aesthetic preferences—my "values," as they say[4]—in the morally and politically relevant customs of the social context in which I happen to live? In other words, does my conscience resonate with the socially incarnated standards of decency?

The answer to this question varies considerably according to the socially dominant ethos of the nation, association, family, or club to which one belongs, and to one's own criteria for discernment and evaluation. Can I, for example, trust a state in which equality of individual rights is the norm? The answer depends on the interpretation of those rights, as expressed pragmatically in its laws and decisions, and my own conception of that equality. I might, for instance, have reservations about giving the same number of votes to a hundred university professors of political theory as to a hundred illiterate citizens. Or I might be angry about a system of taxation that does not combat the growing gap in earnings between the wealthy and the poor.

Can I trust a totalitarian state to provide me with a bearable situation, although it forbids me to practice my own religion, because another religion or, for that matter, atheism, is its official ideology? Perhaps I or my family risk being sent to some gulag. Worse than distrust, continual anguish will fill my life as long as this society continues its tyranny. Do I prefer dying over betraying my conscience? Shall I behave in public as a conformist, hoping that I will be treated as a law-abiding citizen? Or shall I try to combine public obedience with interior opposition?

To live in social distrust, without finding any refuge for living in agreement with my own deep convictions, is certainly an awful form of pressure. The future is constantly threatened and the present must be hidden insofar as it would express what I profoundly am.

In the so-called free world, it is not always permissible to publicly express what one would like to say or do in the intimacy of a home, but most limitations seem reasonable and easy to observe. It is still quite possible to disagree strongly with its generally established and recommended way of life, but as long as we, despite occasional or lingering disagreements, feel sufficiently supported by the police, the legal and judiciary system, taxation, and recourse to elections, our general trust for now and the near future prevails. Even if the common good and one's own well-being as a part of it are not always recognizable in the course of events, a sufficient portion of internal peace, social security and self-realization justifies a basic trust, while the possibility of distrust remains necessary in order to remain and make others alert with regard to symptoms of abuse and corruption.

The proportions of social trust and distrust vary according to the personal standards one has developed. A demanding conscience despises a rich society that considers the poverty of the poor normal, while it distrusts the motivation of those politicians who never have experienced what poverty means, whereas a low standard facilitates bribes and corruption in the police and business (as usual). The distrust of a more suspicious person might thus testify to a higher ethical standard, whereas a person who feels all right in a context of widespread corruption has fewer problems with the situation's degree of trustworthiness.

One could, of course, ask which form of social trust is best, but an answer presupposes that we are able to determine how people should be permitted and stimulated to participate in the forming of a good and historically realizable society. Such a determination has a political and a moral aspect. The personal consciences of the citizens cannot be separated from the political constitution of their union. The first monument of political philosophy in the West, Plato's *Politeia,*[5] has shown this no less than the last of the modern tradition, Hegel's *Philosophy of Right;*[6] but despite many parallels,[7] their climate is quite different. Whereas Plato's ideal is the good-and-beautiful performance of a beautiful-and-good community of noble—truly aristocratic—persons, who live for the harmonious and strong cohesion of their *polis,* Hegel's nation is constructed in the name of rights, mutual obligations, and the universal respectability of all private, particular, and communitarian levels of free self-realization. Both philosophies demonstrate a trustworthy combination of monarchic, oligarchic, and democratic elements at their best under the guidance of philosophical wisdom, but freedom and right demand distance and respect, whereas the beauty of overflowing goodness wants taste and virtuous emulation. Thus both constitutions picture a communal life that is inspired by a single, dominant idea; but beauty and right are not identical, although Plato's and Hegel's pictures of the best *polis* can be read as two modifications of the same ideal. However, Plato shows more awareness of decadent tendencies in private and social life. He therefore insists more strongly on the necessity of alert distrust to prevent an unstoppable decline from the best form of soul and state to their worst, unruly, and chaotic disfigurement, which replaces the peace of an all-encompassing union in shared excellence with the chaotic hell of violence and slavery. Consequently, even Plato's utopia cannot be trusted fully. Not even by himself, because his trust in the ideal is accompanied by a form of distrust that has learned from history. This is the reason why, after his enthusiastic description of the ideal city, he describes the perverted versions of it, from oligarchies and plutocracies to totalitarian tyrannies, as the more realistic products of history.[8]

SOCIAL TRUST AS HOPE

If we, citizens of a more or less successful society, ask ourselves and one another whether we can trust this society, the word "trust" draws our attention in different directions.[9] The meaning emphasized in the former pages was linked to the question of whether our society is a good one from the perspective of the political or common good. Is our community just, focused on the well-being of all the members who compose it, including those who lack opportunities for living well on their own? If not, how then can we make it trustworthy in the eyes of the neglected?

When we have trust in our society, we ask not only whether—on the basis of what it has already shown—it has functioned rather well, but also whether it will continue to do so, and, if it has deficiencies, whether it will be able to correct these. A trustworthy society promises to remain or to become good or better. Do we have valid impressions, reasons, feelings for expecting, with a serious degree of assurance, that the organization of our coexistence and the manners of our cooperation will have a satisfactory future? The turns and twists of world history have sufficiently demonstrated that families, states, and nations cannot count on steady advancement or glory, because none of them can prevent or master unforeseen attacks, conquests, declines, or other socio-political disasters. Radical dependence is documented even on this powerful level of empires and Leviathans.

Modern, emancipated, liberated, autonomous people, and especially the intellectuals among them who like to construct monumental powers in their heads, do not like being confronted by the facts of dependence; they would rather speak about risk and risk *taking,* perhaps because the *taking* sounds more active and self-realizing than the acceptance and the patience required by all that happens to us without giving us any say or control over it. If we cannot trust that the future of our own state, union, or world will be bright, distrust might be preponderant in our mix of justified trust and distrust. In any case, no future is sure enough to promise any kind of paradise.

FOUR

Counting on Nature

We count on nature, and sometimes we call it "Mother Nature" because it produces food, shelter, energy, and all that we need to survive. We are even closer to it than children are to their mothers, because our bodies are integral parts of nature, intensely dependent on its processes and behavior. In a sense, we could perhaps say that we never quit Nature's world, not even when we become humus after death.

MOTHER NATURE

Our relation with nature is ambiguous: we are inside, but at the same time outside; utterly subjected to it, but at the same time able to contemplate it from a distance. We admire its beauty and appreciate the abundance of its enjoyable gifts, but we are terrified by its destructive outbursts. Nature has been idealized as a paradise, but often enough it commits horrendous cruelties.

The earliest records of our civilization show that poets have sung of nature's beauty, whereas its usefulness has been scrutinized, expanded, amended, imitated, and transformed by scholars and engineers. Comfort and beauty are what we expect of nature; but when it turns ugly or hostile, we will fight its threats and attempt to restore its splendor.

Pure nature, untouched by human hands, is difficult to find. Almost everywhere nature shows up in some humanized and socialized form. Landscapes are traversed by highways and seas by ships and tankers for trade and war; forests and mountains are inhabited and deforested for gain; deserts are crossed by caravans and used as landfills or used for experiments with nuclear energy; and empty places are explored by tourists for curiosity's sake or by nations for hegemonic or military purposes. Nature thus is perceived as already filtered through the perspective of those who are interested in it, such as hunters, farmers, scouts, geographers, ethnologists, merchants, companies, or nations.

Nevertheless, nature still makes its proper character known through many phenomena that can be distinguished from their existential and social impact. The changes of temperature according to place and season, the falling snow, recurring thunderstorms, or the fertility of the soil are still experienced as manifestations of a prehumanly given nature, whether they occur in the plains or in a town. Or, to mention more encompassing characteristics, nature continues to reveal itself in the great cosmic regularities, the cyclical change of seasons, the repeated emergence of one generation of animals after the other through birth, maturing, and death. Within its wide horizon, nature offers bearable climates, protected spaces for dwelling, and all sorts of animals and fruits for consumption.

When human beings are numerous, they hardly can survive on such gifts, unless they cooperate with nature by developing techniques of gathering, fishing, hunting, planting, harvesting, inventing tools, cooking, grilling, and so on. They supplement the available means by transforming them into an equipment that better serves their purposes. Thus, at least some primitive kind of technical humanization of nature is inevitable.

It is not difficult to list all the goods that nature has available for human use and consumption, to begin with procreation, birth, and growth into maturity. Nature thus displays an abundance of gifts that can be trusted, if one is smart enough to discover them and, if necessary, to adjust them to one's vital needs. However, nature also has another aspect. Although her benefits condition human survival and enjoyment, she also promises a certain death to each living individual and causes unpredictable but memorable disasters. Is she still a trustworthy mother when she attacks, harms, or kills all that lives through devastating hurricanes, volcanic eruptions, immense inundations, and other calamities? Nature's nurturing beneficence can suddenly turn into blows of awful cruelty. Her accustomed orderliness seems to be interrupted by irregular returns to chaotic destruction.

Instructed by our own experience or the memory of former generations, we waver between trust and distrust regarding such a "mother," who occasionally shows her destructive monstrosity. The threat of her disastrous interventions is another reason why we must develop technical means for keeping her under control. The murderous monster in her must be tamed, domesticated, submitted to a more beneficial direction of nature's history. It necessitates a fight in which vulnerable humans protect themselves against the incredibly powerful whims of natural malevolence.

The relations that bind human existence to nature are complicated. As part of nature (we are bodies) and receivers of its gifts, we are at the same time its virtual victims. Our trust in nature's unbridled generosity is almost complete, but, at the same time, she inspires a constant anxiety and distrust in us with regard to her mostly hidden hostility. Her virtual threat must be prevented—but how? The unpredictability and enormity of its outbreak seems to make an adequate prevention impossible.

In many cultures the regular occurrence of natural phenomena—the normal as well as the exceptional ones—is attributed to a host of superhuman spirits, demons, gods or goddesses, whose specific powers are explained in mythical stories about their relations with one another and with human beings within the natural universe. Often the calamities that happen are related to insults or crimes committed by certain individuals, families, tribes, or towns, which thereby have elicited divine or demonic hostility. In order to find protection against reprisals, reconciliation is then necessary. Reconciliation implies purification, and this was found through the performance of certain rituals, such as the bringing of specific sacrifices or the performance of particular works, which would appease the offended power.

Since the techniques of the time did not suffice to prevent or overcome the threats of nature, liturgical purification and renewed obedience, accompanied by prayer were more important than inefficient attempts at overpowering nature's power directly via merely human means. Consequently, it was extremely important to be in good standing with the supernatural and sacred powers. However, in the end, it was nature itself that, after a disaster, had to return to its more loyal course of events. For nature is its own healer.

To illustrate this in a context removed from the mythical context of ancient rites, we might focus on the trust or distrust deserved by the small piece of nature that our own body represents in each of us: can we trust our bodily well-being, that is, our health? Probably most people trust their own body without often reflecting about the quality of its functioning. We are accustomed to certain corporeal automatisms and confident that they will work normally, unless we have a noticeable handicap or temporary dysfunction. If we become sick or disabled, the doctor gives advice, we use a medication or undergo an operation, but neither the doctor nor the surgeon nor I myself, nor the medication nor the operation heals me. It is nature itself, concretized in this (still) living body, which must heal itself, although the required interventions may ease the healing process.

On the more encompassing level of, for example, a fatal deluge, we can see a parallel to the individual body's course from health, through sickness or dysfunction, toward a renewed phase of health. Similarly, after an inundation, the customary course of the river returns to its normal regime—with, sometimes, a variation. A long time of trusting nature's course, interrupted by a terrible reversal of its customary trustworthiness, is followed by a new, less naïve and more cautious phase of trust, mixed with suspicion and qualified distrust. Similarly, the trust that makes us confident about the service our body usually delivers, is never a certainty. It is, for example, possible that I will awaken tomorrow to find that my writing arm is paralyzed.

If we consider all the possibilities, it is amazing that we are not more worried than we are. Are we sensitive enough to realize that possible harm, pain, dying, death, and accidents are around every corner? But we must defend ourselves against constant anxiety by a trust that, on the whole and for the most part, things will be okay. Ignorance and indifference or illusions in many varieties can certainly function as tactics of reassurance, but don't they falsify the meaning of human life, which is a dangerous one? And who can remain ignorant of the recent deluges in Asia?

MODERN TECHNOLOGY

The technological conquests of the last centuries have changed the face of the earth. Canalization and dams to divert the course of rivers, leveling of mountains and changing deserts into gardens, covering the world with highways and industrial parks, building forms of the highest possible towers and many other monumental constructions have made nature's original appearance almost unrecognizable. Technology has even begun to penetrate the planetary space.

Is the great technological project of our era a straightforward continuation of the human attempt to domesticate nature, so that it becomes more docile to our wants and wishes, more friendly to humankind, better adjusted to the course of human history—and consequently more trustworthy for humankind? Our technology seems to be inspired by a spirit of its own. Its character, not only its enormity, is particular.

With regard to the question of trust and distrust in nature, some important differences between the premodern relations of humankind to nature and the technological attitude of our era must be noted. Our epoch no longer approaches nature as a mother in a mixture of gratitude and fear, but rather as an inexhaustible mass of matter and materials that we can handle, use, change, transmute, posses, sell, and buy as we like. Nothing is left of the veneration that was expressed in the mythical interpretation according to which natural phenomena are obedient to benevolent or malevolent deities; but even a certain respect for nature's wonderful abundance in fertility, energy, life-giving and life-restoring power seems to have evaporated. When the technological approach becomes absolute, nature's data are no longer treated as gifts from the gods or from nature's own prolific generosity; instead they just form a huge reservoir of things and stuff: elementary material that can be studied and changed into objects. Nature is then no longer approached in a "dative" mode, because it is reduced to an objective reality in the strong sense of objectivity.[1] The question of trust or distrust in nature has consequently become moot.

When nature is reduced to the material totality of all that can be found, grasped, appropriated, studied, dissected, assembled, reconstructed, produced, reproduced, bought, and sold, the question of trust makes place for another question: What do we want to make of it and how shall we use it? Objectifying theory and utilitarian forms of *praxis* and *poeisis* are then the reactions that fit nature's mode of showing up.

Making, producing, taking full possession and control of the available material in order to make it completely conform to our wishes—seem to be the ideal of a mindset obsessed by domination over a reality that unexpectedly can show itself refractory. Is this the ideal of contemporary technology? Is this ideal expressed, for example, in the mass production of chicken, milk, and cows? If so, nature seems to have changed from being "Mother Nature" to nature as a product of human (all too human?) work, made by human engineering on the basis of the available elements. If this idea were realized in all parts and aspects of nature, humanity would have substituted its own product for the motherly (and terrifying) nature that was given to us without any effort of our own.

As we will see in chapter 6, Descartes formulated the grand project of an all-encompassing philosophy as conceptual reconstruction of the universe, starting from scratch and finishing with a complete theory of ethics, mechanics, and medicine. Is the technological (re)production of a more humane nature the practical parallel to that theoretical project?

The natural sciences, which during the last centuries have brilliantly developed their insights, are proud—and from their own perspective rightly so—of their objective, wholly impartial and unbiased (but mathematically framed) relation to their subject matters. Their purpose implies that scholars should not be personally involved in the material—elements, plants, animals, or human bodies—they study, because involvement spoils objectivity. By observing their objects—a sample of water, a rose, a corpse, a cow, or a human body, for example—and submitting them to their experiments, they prepare them for scientific analysis and conceptual reconstruction. If they discover that a modification of the given structure or the properties of the studied objects would yield a more satisfactory result than the existing ones, they would like, in cooperation with specialized engineers, to change these objects. Making better objects than the ones that are given by nature is then a normal consequence.

Is engineering the practical parallel to the theoretical framework of modernity?[2] Both fit well into the ideal of autonomy, if this may be interpreted as the independence of someone who, from the top, oversees the universe as displayed and available for his or her attention, investigation, evaluation, and reordering. Obviously, this imaginary stance is the opposite of a humiliated or humble acceptance of an almost total dependence on nature's course. But it is also different from a negotiated trust, mixed with distrust, which gratefully, but somewhat diffidently, adheres to nature in the expectation that it, on the whole, will take care of us as long as it is not time to die.

In its most extreme unfolding, the person who stays on top would imagine him- or herself not only able to correct but also to reshape and even to remake nature. The primitive, not yet humanized nature of creation should be replaced by a more satisfactory one. The modern technologist would then be a Promethean re-creator whose work surpasses the primitive form of nature by a more efficient and more enjoyable kind of sophistication.

Our questions about trust in nature would then change into the question of whether we can put our confidence in the remakes produced by those who prefer a second nature. The answer depends, of course, on the purpose and the taste of the (re)makers. For example, is it better for us to consume bread and fruit drinks with or without large quantities of added sugar? Or is it good for the world to build production systems that stimulate "the economy," while grossly polluting water, earth, air, and light?

Humankind has greatly profited from the enormous advances, in all kinds of technology, that resulted from the splendid conquest of the modern sciences. The massive humanization of innumerable natural processes—from procreation, via childcare, healing of the sick, feeding the hungry, and communication between all parts of the globe, to alleviation of suffering and prevention of unnecessary deaths—has been a blessing. Human practice has supplemented the capabilities of nature's motherly qualities. But in the end, it is nature itself that has the last word, when birth, survival, growth, healing, and death are at stake. In this sense nature deserves a deep but cautious trust.

FIVE

Self-Confidence

Chapter 2 approached the phenomenon of interpersonal trust through the simple model of my entrusting you with a certain task. When reflecting on the phenomenon of self-confidence, can we approach it by adapting the structure of "my entrusting you" to my own trusting (or distrusting) *myself* as the one who—instead of you, him, her, them, all of you, or us—accomplishes a task or work that has to be done? If so, can I explain the structure of self-confidence or trust in myself as a trust of which I am the origin or the subject, while I am *also* the person "in the dative" to whom I confide a work that I want to be accomplished or that has been asked of or imposed on me?

CAN I TRUST MYSELF?

If so, the first necessary modification of the analysis given in chapter 2 is, of course, that the relation between two persons (for example, you—or she—and me) be replaced by one person who has an internal relation to this same person. This presupposes a distance between me (I) and myself (I), but at the same time a difference between the

I who wants a task to be accomplished and imposes it on me, and the I that must accomplish the task and thereby realizes what I want. I want *me* to accomplish what I want. I want myself *as* fulfilling my wanting; or I want to do what I want to be done by me. I want myself as active in realizing a certain work, which involves myself as wanting this realization. When I ask whether I can trust myself with regard to this event, the *me* that is trusted is, as trusted, not exactly the same I or me as the one that *does* the trusting. On the other hand, it cannot be another person, because it is my own self that, as wanting and willing, spurs itself to accomplish what I will.

But how, then, do I differ from myself in this relationship? My identity (with myself) is functionally dual: as wanting—and then as trusting or distrusting—I take a distance from myself insofar as I address myself as the I that is working (but also wanting—and trusting or distrusting—its own operation).

Let us first focus on the self that is trusted or not (by the self that trusts it or not). What is at stake here? At least two properties: Is the self *capable* of performing what it has to do, and is it *willing* to do so?

When someone asks me to write a book on trust, I suppose that this person has enough trust in my having the capabilities that are required for indeed writing such a book. She shows her trust by entrusting me with it, but she is not sure whether I will accept the task. Depending on several uncertain factors, she might hope or trust or expect that I will accept the task, but she cannot predict whether I will agree and indeed *want* to perform the work. My will is uncertain, although she might know me so well that she trusts that I indeed will accept the responsibility for it. My capabilities (or, in other words, the skills required for the wanted work) and the decision of my will are both required to make a deal or sign a contract. In signing a contract, however, I not only agree with the will of the entrusting other, but I also bind my own will and the mobilization of my skills, insofar as they are required, to the obligation that from then on governs my working on the projected task.

A task is not always contracted or entrusted; it can be a self-imposed task, which then, before or after my taking it on me, may prompt the question: can I do it? Am I able to bring this task to a successful end and will I, when difficulties arise, be stubborn enough to will its continuation? In other words: can I trust myself as *capable* and *willing* with regard to this work? Will the book I am writing be good enough? Will it satisfy my own criteria and those of the commissioner?

Before continuing the analysis of the double I on which I am focusing, I must remind the reader of a classical distinction that might clarify this difficult relation.

In his *Ethics,* Aristotle distinguishes two generic types of human activities: *poiēsis* and *praxis. Poiēsis* has to do with *making* and the production of a work (*ergon*), for example a poem or a computer. The examples used in chapter 2 belong to the world of *poiēsis. Praxis,* however, is an activity that changes the active person him- or herself, without producing a product, thing, instrument, or work outside this person, who instead affects, changes, performs, or displays him- or herself. Dancing or performing in an opera are examples of it. If we take *praxis* or performance in a very broad sense, which encompasses an entire life, we focus on the general and total performance of a life from conception to death. Living or "practicing" a human life coincides with the entire course of a singular person as long as it moves.

No one can refuse to live, because suicide is no refusal, but a self-chosen performance of life's last stage. Consequently, we are always doing, performing, or practicing what we *are.* This is a nonchosen but purely given task, for which Aristotle uses *also* the word *ergon* (work), but now as the summary of a praxis that coincides with each individual's life as to be lived. All the specific works a person might have to accomplish in the course of his or her existence are then seen as moments or phases of an ongoing adventure, for which the involved person has the final responsibility in cooperation with the many persons and circumstances whose influences cannot be avoided.

The analysis of trust with regard to some entrusted work, given above, can be modified by shifting our focus from particular tasks to the existential task of living one's own life without restriction to any of its projects or periods. Can I trust myself as involved in and responsible for my own entire life? The necessity of living my own life—more than just the realization of a particular, voluntarily accepted or chosen task—is, of course, the main "work" I must accomplish, but it imposes a huge demand on me: I must perform my life responsibly and well. The entirety of its run must, all in all, be good. A satisfactory explanation of the implications contained in this command belongs to a complete ethics, but here we can only mention a few snippets of such an ethics, insofar as they are relevant for trust and distrust.

CAN I TRUST THAT I WILL LIVE WELL?

Who could answer this question? The entirety of an individual life cannot be evaluated before it is finished; but death takes away the person before she can ask whether her life has been a good one. Before we pass the threshold between life and death, we cannot *know* whether our life, as a whole, was a good life. In the last minute, we might have an impression, but there is no time left to draw a well-documented conclusion.[1] As long as we are not agonizing, however, we must delay an answer. But, being still alive, can't I have a kind of global trust about myself that encourages me to a certain optimism regarding the rest of my life? Or should I recognize that my past and present way of life rather suggests distrust with regard to my future?

That I cannot *know* how I will have lived when I will die, is due to several factors. In the first place, all futures are uncertain. Most prognoses and predictions are refuted because so many natural, economic, political, and cultural surprises and disasters happen, while our own corporeal, mental, and spiritual processes and experiences may change unexpectedly. Will we remain the same, loyal to our present orientation, as healthy as today, as sharp and skillful, as much a mixture of virtues and vices, and so on? Will we keep our composure in the dire circumstances of war, occupation, epidemic, or famine? If we cannot know the answer to such questions because both the historical circumstances and our own attitude may change considerably, even cautious trust, based on my personal experience of the already performed and familiar past, seems too risky. But is there an alternative?

No one can live without at least a minimal degree of confidence, and insofar as this confidence regards my own behavior, it is supported by my own experiences of a past that encompasses the normal behavior of the people I met, the regular processes of nature, social life and culture, my own corporeal, emotional, intellectual, and spiritual actions and reactions, and the personal patterns through which I have adjusted myself to the world in which I move. By basing my judgment on this ensemble of regularities, while also asking myself how I would act in extraordinary, or even horrendous, circumstances, I have formed a very global, but unclear and provisional expectation regarding my own personal future. I certainly simplify the situation by not considering the mistakes I might make and the disasters that can happen to me, but what I know of personal histories seems to confirm the impression that most individuals remain the same in character and demeanor, although some pass through dramatic crises or conversions.

If it is not possible to evaluate my life before it is dead, I still can ask, and perhaps answer with a high degree of probability, how I will be in the near future or even later, if my surroundings or history do not change dramatically. Because many conditions must be realized, such questions cannot be answered without reservations, however. If, for example, I am involved in the lengthy preparation of a project or an ideal to which I want to dedicate the best years of my life, I must have some trust about the life I will live later, during the time in which I will be a teacher of mathematics, a dentist, a farmer, and how I will behave as a mother, a friend, or a hermit. The question about trusting myself becomes then a more restricted one: What sort of trust can I have regarding my own future on the basis of my familiarity with myself-as-I-have-become-until-now? My past, insofar as I am acquainted with it, provides me with a partial and unfinished experience, in which I am at once the personal past I remember, the not yet realized future me, whom I try to imagine as prolongation of my past, and the present I, who asks: "Will I, can I become what I now would like to be?" Can I say: "I *trust* that I will be such"? *Hope* would be a more adequate word:

"I *hope* that I become what I would like to be." Are there in fact strong reasons for doubting such a future? Then I must perhaps distrust what I like. Or else I should solve the discordance between my possibilities and the desire that motivates my self-projection.

WHICH I GIVES THE ANSWER?

It is obvious that the question of self-trust remains implicit in the practice of many individuals. Self-confidence or its contrary are not often generated as conclusions of an explicit examination of one's past. Most often confidence or diffidence, like assurance or self-doubt, remain on the level of feelings or moods that support or disturb our behavior.

We must turn to the psychologists to hear how the nuances and degrees of trust and distrust in oneself vary according to the various stages of life and the types of experience elicited by different functions and professions. Being old and close to death stimulates reflection about one's past and interest in a correct evaluation of its merits and debts, but the number of new tasks to be accomplished has diminished. The future has become short and the question of whether one can still trust one's own body and spirit to finish life in a more or less fruitful and gratifying way cannot be brushed away. Remembering past actions and omissions, successes obtained and failures, the guilt accumulated and the signs of recognition that come to mind might result in a balance of trust and distrust about the memory one leaves, but death itself seems the greater threat. Is all self-trust made moot by death? Can't we stop desiring, hoping, reaching out beyond death toward some more or less trustworthy form of being saved and alive: some posterity perhaps, a name, a legacy, or even a mysteriously transmuted revival of my singular destiny?

For infants, the future of their behavior is hardly a problem; self-reflection is not a frequent activity for them until they notice the first symptoms of a personal conscience. However, as soon as children are trained in social and professional skills, they learn that one cannot live without adequate habits and a trustworthy manner of participating in the human society. They then also learn to check their own progress in adaptation and reliability.

Learning how to live a fully human life on all the essential—socially and morally acceptable, skillful, aesthetic, and religious—levels of humanity remains each one's program until death, but there are periods in which personal confrontation with one's own trustworthiness takes on a special importance, because one's growth into adult responsibility demands individual emancipation.

Once adult and established as a relatively independent citizen, one cannot avoid the question of whether one's habits and overall manner of life deserve the trust of partners, friends, colleagues, pupils—or rather distrust, at least in some respects that must be corrected. Can I sincerely state for myself that I am trustworthy in all that I do or say? The criterion to which I appeal for a truthful answer depends on my conscience (which might have been refined or distorted by slogans or well-instructed by means of a good education). I can and must, from time to time, ask my conscience, whether I can trust it or whether I rather should have it cleaned up because it has been poisoned by seductive pleasures or bad ideologies. Those persons who have to deal with me on a regular basis, have a spontaneous opinion about my qualities, not only with regard to a particular task, but also to my general sincerity and demeanor. Some of them might be good judges, but none of them knows all my intentions or the hidden failures that left their shame in me. I myself am the best-placed person to judge the degree of my trustworthiness, but am I unprejudiced enough to be a trustworthy judge?

This, again, is the twofold structure of the self. I am the person who is aware of this same person's past and present and possible future praxis, which includes not only external behavior, but also my secret ideas and motivations. As aware of my own praxis, I judge and evaluate it, but according to which criteria? The question I must ask and answer, is not only "Am I—the judging I—impartial?" but also "Where does the judging I take or find the trustworthy measure or the 'law' that should guide my own evaluation of this (my own) life that appears in my court?" We call the moral aspect of the judge's consciousness—its inner law or standard—*conscience.* But all consciences have been formed and reformed during our growing up and thereafter. Each individual's conscience has been guided and influenced by various instructors, who, in turn, were influenced by various traditions. Did all these influences have only salutary or also distorting effects? One powerful influence comes from the dominant ethos of our milieu and most of us have accepted that ethos as a valid law for good behavior. Full responsibility, however, demands that I personally check whether the ethos I inherited from my surrounding community truly is the right and unadulterated standard I need for pronouncing a fair judgment about my own conscience, which, until my moral awakening, adheres to the average morality of a certain culture or subculture. I, my singular self, thus am not only the behaving I (my life as it unrolls before my self-conscious and conscientious I) but also a supraconscientious I that is aware of my own possibly flattened, tainted, distorted, falsified, or treacherous conscience. Once I have discovered the difference between a socially recommended conscience (the generally celebrated "values") and the necessity of a fully true supra- or metaconscience (or "law" of all laws), the question of a correct, pure, and good standard of all standards—one that is not only socially recommended—can no longer be suppressed.

Where, when, and how does this highest conscience reveal itself? We trust that it somehow is present in our self, because our suspicions about the average ethos and our own obedience to it seem to come from the inside. But perhaps we need wise or saintly persons to discover what our most inner voice reveals. Can we be confident that our conscience will become more sensitive and truthful, if it uses its suspicions about its own judgments for a purification of its highest standards?

CHOOSING

For a fully true judgment one should, of course, also be informed about all the facts and forces that have determined the praxis at stake.

In the context of this chapter this praxis is my own life, as it has developed until now. But what do we know and what should we know about an individual in order to pronounce a fair judgment about his or her own part in the result? Some people are quick in declaring that I am or have become what I have chosen to be, as if no other causes than individual liberty were responsible for the way my habits turn out to be.

Whatever one might think about the possibility of choices, many all-important determinations are neither choosable nor annullable. For example, the fact that you and I exist, that each of us is born at an unchangeable date from two other, equally contingent individuals, that we cannot undo the facts of our pasts (although their meaning still may be modified), that death will take each living person away from human history, and—to speak the language of the philosophical tradition—that human nature structures and characterizes our actions. At the beginning of our lives, we are not able to choose any of the factors that later will have a decisive impact on our characters and careers: the language and culture of the society into which we are introduced by these particular parents, the religion and ideas of the specific epoch, the climate and the beauty or ugliness of the country that offers us the first impressions of a homeland, and the unpredictable wars and crises of history.

Do those who refer so often to choosing and free choice—most of which are predictable because most people do, like, consume, and buy what everybody else does and likes—forget all the determinations that have shaped us before the first expression of a will of our own could appear? We always arrive too late on the world scene to intervene in the complicated convergence of a thousand forces and facts that have already shaped our destiny long before we become aware of their result. The mistake of much speculation lies in the illusion that the freedom of human beings consists in the possibility of starting all over again from a blank, wholly undetermined, situation that would permit us to construct an ideal way of life from almost nothing, as if learning how to live well could be invented on the basis of a Cartesian abstraction from real history or according to a *modus geometricus* in the style of Spinoza. In fact, practically all features of our early life were already determined and we had no other choice than to accept what we got. It is only later that chances are offered to intervene and to cooperate with influential persons and events that accompany or surround us. But even then our interventions and the strictly conditioned moments of choice that are granted us are caught in a fate that is composed of inevitable constraints together with societal and individual initiatives.

What does this entanglement of freedom with necessity mean for the questions of trust and trustworthiness?

To trust or distrust myself-as-I-have-become after a number of years, I ask myself whether my present way of life, as the result of a complicated convergence of my cooperation with many other persons, forces, events, and processes, justifies confidence, suspicion, caution, distrust, or concern with respect to the continuation of my life, which, I hope, will be granted on similar conditions as the ones that marked my past. I could, however, be surprised or shocked, as many people have been in the past. Caution and at least a small degree of distrust belong therefore to any realistic trust. We are neither gods nor counselors of God. Destiny and fate are part of human singularity.

A FEW THESES ABOUT TRUST AND DEPENDENCE

Trust in oneself is not an easy topic for reflection. The selfhood of the self (you, I, he, she), including its inconvertible singularity and situated originarity, is highly controversial among philosophers. I will not try to solve the enigmas that surround "the ego" or "me" and "I myself," but I have tried to indicate briefly how the question of my trustworthiness entangles us in several other problems. For further meditation, I note here only a few, perhaps too boldly stated, theses, which could trigger much discussion if we had the time and the space to make self-confidence the sole focus of this book.

(1) I depend in all that I say, do, think, and wish on others, who are equally dependent on others. Dependence without trust creates anguish and this intensifies distrust.

(2) That all egos are able to exist, develop, enact, and express themselves, they owe to the society and the culture that forms them.

Trust is the default position, but disruptive experiences may generate and foster distrust.

(3) I am myself and have my own manners and style in all that I do.

(4) I do not possess myself, however. My self is not a kind of property, but the main condition and driving origin of all appropriation. I can be grateful for this self, just as I can be grateful for existing, but I never am, nor can become its master. The self in me is not sovereign, because it is driven by a desire that I can neither choose nor abolish. Without having chosen it, I *am* this desire: obsessed by a drive or pathos that cannot stop my reaching out to an unknown but fulfilling mode of being myself perfectly alive. If I can trust this pathos, my life is oriented, but the desired orientation might remain hidden to my intelligence, although it suggests trust.

(5) My self is the primary promise of a successful life, but in its realization, it is also a burden, which makes me suffer. For both success and suffering *well* I am responsible.

(6) I cannot accomplish the task (or "work"[2]) of my life without association with others, on whom I rely. I welcome this dependence insofar as it makes my own life possible. To be a *real* (that is, realized and developed) self, I must let others participate in the unfolding of my life. Their trust in me and my trust in them transforms certain elements of their lives, words, convictions, and actions into elements of my existence. We mutually unite and participate in shared existences and this builds mutual trust.

(7) The others' selfhood shines in their faces and targets me through their eyes. Their existence in front of me alerts me to their commanding dignity. What they *are* as singular persons *demands* from me that I care for them and accept co responsibility for their lives. Their selves *summon* me to welcome and serve their true interests. That I am able to exercise this dedication is due to those earlier others who have welcomed me and taught me how to live, when I was not yet free enough to take also my own responsibility for it. By doing so, they have awakened my will and therewith opened my possibility and necessity of trusting and distrusting.

(8) My existence—concretized in my past as oriented to the future of others and myself as one of them *and* as a singular destiny—advances in gratitude for the past of my ongoing adventure. The present, in which their and my past sets out for a common and individually different future, would not be possible if it were not carried, supported, and encouraged by a trust that is at least as strong as the fear that is inspired by the many risks that threaten our fragile existence.

HUMILITY OR ARROGANCE

Self-confidence is not the same as arrogance. If trust in my own possibilities includes a correct evaluation of the properties, habits, accomplishments, and products I have shown in my recent past, this justifies my trust that I will perform similarly well in the near future—unless I have already detected symptoms of debilitation.

The preceding pages have emphasized a host of personal and social conditions on which each individual has to count in order to become a capable and trustworthy person. It would be possible to write an encyclopedic work on all the persons, things, institutions, circumstances, and events that make us dependent during each phase of our existence, and such would be a healthy exercise in realizing how little I myself have contributed to what I now have become. Not only my corporeal well-being, my eating and drinking habits, my emotional patterns, my technical and intellectual skills, and my entire spiritual formation were conditioned by innumerable contributions of other persons and fortunate circumstances; but my existence as such and the bare but basic fact of its continuation are purely given, without any effort on my part. Or could I, by any chance, claim a power of self-creation?

The depth and compass of our dependencies are mind-boggling. It shows how necessary and how extensive it was to trust the conditions of what I have become. And this necessity keeps accompanying my life, as long as it moves forward. For, to begin with, how can I have plans or make any promise if I do not count on remaining capable of executing what I want or promise to do, if I do not trust that I will be there to do it? When I answer you, "Yes, I will do that tomorrow," I trust that tomorrow I will be alive and able to do what I promise you today. But who can guarantee this fact? In any case, I do not have any provable certainty about it. My trust in my own living on is stronger than the entire range of doubts that could be spelled out about the continuation of my very existence. Trust trumps doubts and many anxieties, whereas distrust underlines the precariousness of our radical dependence on powers that escape our might and choice.

By emphasizing our very profound dependence, trust gets rid of many illusions about personal autonomy. Insofar as I am involved in decisions about my future, my freedom emerges from an already mannered life, for which other persons and powers were more responsible than I myself. Insofar as I consider my own style of life fortunate because it permits me to live in an approvable way, I owe gratitude to those who "made" me. But why do we take their contributions for granted and why are we inclined to forget those who were responsible for our existence and its formation?

Trust testifies to our dependence; it implies gratitude for the present result of a cooperative past and hope that things will continue to function well. But trust also humbles. It refutes anyone who believes to be the origin of his own life and attributes, as if he were his own mother, father, nurse, and educator, or even a self-creating god.

Arrogance is the illusion of individual sovereignty. Pride about the bit of originality I may have contributed to my growth in corporeal and spiritual maturity is justified on the same grounds as gratitude to the many others who have contributed the rest; but boasting on all received, borrowed, or stolen parts, as if they were my own creation, is ridiculous. An arrogant person feels humiliated when all the details of his past and present dependence are spelled out, because his ego takes up too much space to recognize the role of benefactors. Not only does he imagine himself to be the origin and center of his life; he acts as if he is also the center of his universe. One could call him a transcendental ego, somewhat analogically to the Ego that some Idealists promoted as the beginning and the end of their system. But arrogance does not understand that egocentrism is a prison. All interests converge thereby into a self that converts all otherness into the private property of a sovereign but singularly narrow and phantasmatic *causa sui* without friends.

A humble person, on the contrary, recognizes his overall dependence as a fact. He has learned that acceptance is at least as important as originality and that most of his best ideas and ideals are borrowed from predecessors, who made available what they, in cooperation with others, had appropriated and redistributed. The humble mind is much wider and richer than the arrogating one because it is more hospitable to suggestions and proposals. Free from the obsession of its own sufficiency, its horizon tends to be universal, so that others are welcome to present their own findings in it. Trust in others and in one's own dependence on them goes very well together with openness, gratitude, hospitality, and sharing, while egoism is arrogant, lost in illusions, imprisoned in solitude, and repetitious in idiosyncrasies.

Trusting my own ability to perform my given life decently does not slip into arrogance, if it is permeated by the recognition of all the gifts that I have received and appropriated with the help of innumerable benefactors. Instead of being obsessed by its singular preeminence and fame, it enjoys and praises the many conditions and conditioners that contributed to ego's own possibility.

CAN I TRUST MY ORIENTATION?

If *ego* is not its own god, what then is its goal, meaning, ideal, or most desirable reality? What provides my life with its overarching orientation?

A human life is driven by a host of needs and desires, thus pushing us in various directions. Many desires compete and contradict one another, which forces us to pacify their conflicts by limiting their often exorbitant claims. In the name of which standard or ideal can we harmonize their contentious claims? Is there one preferable, encompassing, surpassing, final, or transcending end or ideal that we want more and above anything else, that is, beyond all other *desiderata* that attract us?

Since the beginning of civilization, people have sought and thought about the meaning of what they experienced as the Desire that does not coincide with any of their particular needs (for food, sex, play, entertainment, comfort, and so on) or desires (of seeing and making beauty or being recognized, respected, loved, forgiven, and so on). That Desire is at the same time more vague and more promising than all our particular needs and desires together. Beautiful names, like *eudaimonia* (being well disposed by a good demon), *beatitudo* (beatitude, bliss), *salud, felicità, bonheur, geluk, or Glückseligkeit* (the bliss of being fortunate) have been given to the target of that Desire, but all these words, and most of all the English word *happiness,* have lost their luster by being applied to an ensemble of all ordinary *desiderata* and pleasures.

That we are driven toward a culmination of desirability beyond all the particular satisfactions that can be enjoyed during a mortal life, is an empirical fact. Equally certain, however, is the fact that we cannot stop asking, without however receiving a clear answer, what and how the ultimate *Desideratum* might be, and that the absence of a reply makes us suffer. We want to know what, in the end—and consequently also from the beginning—gives our existence its dynamic impulse to embrace the life that we never chose but discover as already driven and intending beyond the multiplicity of desires that capture our immediate or periodic attention. We want to know what gives us an ultimate and decisive orientation.[3]

What we *know* about it is rather formal and abstract. It surpasses the totality of the multiple drives that divide our purposes and plans of action; but it is not a genus of which this dynamic multiplicity is a specification. The satisfaction it promises is not mixed with any dissatisfaction and it does not slip or die away, as other satisfactions do. What we know of its qualities is mostly negative: the ultimate Desirable that orients us is not comparable to any other *desideratum*—it is not just nice, pleasant, delicious, valuable, admirable, like masterpieces or blissful hours with lovable persons—but, on the other hand, blissful moments and peak experiences of beauty or greatness, wonderful gestures and words of compassion or reconciliation have more symbolic force than other events in pointing toward a final destination that would make us completely fortunate. Do these indications convince us that the human dynamism is determined by a radical and incomparable orientation, which has not waited for our approval to mobilize and motivate our lives? Perhaps we are not able to understand this orientation, but, because we can neither change nor escape from it, we might as well follow the radical Desire, which gives our existence its ineradicable direction.

All religions have developed myths and stories about the radical orientation that determines the ultimate meaning of human life. They help us to imagine—and then also to somewhat understand—what really counts and how we can translate our "natural" (or essential) orientation into travel guides for walking through the stages of a well-performed life.

Do we need religion to be convinced of the demands that issue from our main orientation? Can philosophy or common sense replace the myths and messages that offer us guidance? Or is a spontaneous kind of trust—even without understanding—sufficient for living a peaceful life, despite the many riddles and dissatisfactions of all earthly endeavors?

One has the impression that most people—and especially those who live in peace with themselves and others—silently agree with their own "heart," insofar as this is guided by its own, not chosen, but radical and relentless Desire. Their agreement is a question of trust—a trust that often is fed, strengthened and concretized by religious imagination and participation in collective celebrations of revealing events, but the same or a similar trust in our original and ultimate Desire might also awaken on its own, thanks to the irrepressible generosity of its Orient.

The difference between the transcendence of Desire and the arrogance of all attempts at sovereignty is the difference between heaven and hell. Trust in one's own unavoidable Desire is the basic form of acceptance, whereas arrogance tries desperately to refute the all-encompassing condition of its own possibility by imagining that the self chooses its ownmost originary goal and movement. How could it be the source of its end and beginning—and thus also of its own dynamic essence? Eros frees the self from a sovereign boredom to which nothing really new happens. Dare we trust that our basic pathos does not drive us in vain? Do we dare to trust the lead of our own mysterious orientation?

PART III: Trust in Philosophy and Religion

Parts 1 and 2 have sketched the formal structure of trusting as entrusting someone with a specific task (chapters 1 and 2) and asked how this structure must be modified when we direct our trust or distrust toward three domains that we can neither avoid nor wholly distrust. Indeed, we are involved and integrated parts of the society (chapter 3), of nature (chapter 4), and of our own subjectivity (chapter 5). Together, these domains form the universe of which each science studies an aspect, but from its beginning philosophy has claimed to be interested in the totality of all beings (*ta panta*), which it collects as a universe (*to pan* [cf. Parmenides, Fragment B and Plato, Sophist, 244b–e, 245b–d]).

Is the universe that which we must recognize as the primordial foundation of all trust or is this impossible because it lacks perfect trustworthiness? Chapters 6 and 7 point out that this question has been answered differently in modern and medieval philosophy. These rapid sketches serve here as an introduction to a discussion of the basic and ultimate question: Should we, in the end and from the beginning invest our trust in the universe itself or follow a desire that transcends the horizon of the universe toward a noncomposed but absolutely unique origin and end beyond (the) all?

SIX

Trust in Philosophy

What is the relevance of trust for philosophy as it is practiced in our century? The question is not often thematized, but it is answered, at least implicitly, by the philosophical praxis, and especially by all teachers who introduce beginning students into the ongoing history of the worldwide realm called philosophy. To become acquainted with this realm, one needs not only intelligence, passion, and a good deal of stubborn courage, but also a lot of trust. Indeed, novice philosophers are not yet capable of philosophically justifying a correct judgment about the competence of their teachers. They risk being disappointed. They might have followed the advice of friends, magazines, former students, or high school teachers, but instead of relying on thoroughly probed arguments and unshakeable insights, they rely on their own trust in the opinions of their advisors. Because a bad start can cause a disastrous manner of thinking, they might have prepared their choice of the best available (and affordable) guidance very carefully, but a good deal of trust must have completed the ensemble of reasons that led to their decision.

Are well-formed and advanced philosophers so well-established and rationally certified in their philosophical practice that they have reached complete independence? This is the case, if they have personally demonstrated not only their self-discovered theses and arguments, but also the arguments and conclusions on which they rely without having them fully probed and found obvious. However, this condition seems too difficult. Show me one philosopher whose oeuvre proves everything it affirms. Or, if you think it sufficient that philosophers prove only the correctness of their method, show me one who has been able to do this. All philosophers borrow from predecessors or from certain opinions, convictions, dogmas, or beliefs that, in their surroundings or the inner circle of their specialty, are generally considered true, even if rigorous proofs are lacking. Insofar as I have been able to study the arguments that support some of the classics of philosophy—such as the works of Plato, Descartes, Spinoza, Kant, and Hegel—their admirable unfolding contains several fundamental affirmations whose plausibility or beauty has not been certified by irrefutable proof. Despite their originality and impressive coherence, those works testify to their authors' trust in positions that had to be critically checked and transformed or rejected by thinkers of later times.

Besides much trust in the philosophy of selected predecessors, most philosophers show also trust and belief in some dominant ethos of their own space and time, even if this ethos radically differs from the beliefs that dominate other places or epochs. Not only in politics or economy, but also in philosophy, many participants act as if endless and massive repetitions of popular hypotheses (often called *axioms*) make these hypotheses true, even if no one has been able to prove their rational validity.

An example of this state of affairs is the (nowadays) almost uncontested affirmation of the moral and legal validity of "human rights," which, during the last two centuries, has become a central part of the moral and social ideology of the West. I have not found any noncircular proof for this doctrine, but no philosopher would want or dare to deny it as foundational for contemporary ethics. Another example is the general and uncontested belief in the existence and most fundamental relevance of God's existence, which, for two millennia dominated the European civilization until its slow decline between the fifteenth and the twentieth centuries.

We may state that trust is a basic constituent of any philosophy, and especially of its ethical part, where it comes closest to the existential needs of human life. Notwithstanding this state of affairs, however, the standard initiation of new members into the philosophical realm ignores or rejects the necessity of trust in the name of a dogma according to which autonomy of individual thinking is the distinctive shibboleth of authentic philosophy. Think on your own! Do not believe what *they*—your parents, teachers, heroes, churches, or traditions—tell you. Each person has the capacity, the right, and the duty to examine, criticize, discover, and declare the truth independently. Emancipation, independence, autonomy—often called freedom—are the norm. "You yourself must decide what counts. Do not—like medieval believers—sheepishly follow theological powers that claim to possess a higher wisdom than philosophy!"

In order to better understand—and then also to criticize—such calls for philosophical independence, I want to remind you of Descartes's renewal of philosophy, which may be seen as paradigmatic for the ideal—or myth—of an authentic, modern, and truly postmedieval philosophy.

DESCARTES'S PROGRAM OF A NEW, CERTAIN, AND AUTONOMOUS PHILOSOPHY

In his *Discourse on Method* (1637), Descartes sketches the program of a completely new departure and procedure in philosophy. Indeed, philosophy needs a new basis, one that is a rock of unshakeable certainty, on which rigorous demonstrations can be built according to obvious and certain principles. The entire past of philosophy, with its endless controversies, should be forgotten because it offers no more than a multiplicity of uncertain and mutually contradictory philosophies, none of which rises above the level of probability.

Because the new method demands the discovery of an indubitable and fundamental point of departure, the philosopher must begin by doubting and ignoring all thoughts, perceptions, suggestions and theories that have not yet been shown to be either immediately certain or to follow logically from such evidence. This exclusion encompasses all the opinions, beliefs, convictions, faiths, customs, and assumptions whose claims to truth or validity are not yet certified by the new philosophy that still must be developed. It thus excludes also the generally accepted rules of common sense and the entire ethos that guides the daily lives of average citizens, philosophers and scientists included.

Certainty can be expected from theory only, and theory should be scientific.[1] In order to begin again, a philosopher must give up his being-at-home-in-the-world, insofar as the truth and decency of such hominess is not yet justified, certified, and insured by unshakable evidence and undeniable principles. Using the metaphor of a house, Descartes states that a true philosopher who has not yet proved the whole of truth must dwell in two houses at the same time: the house of his existential concerns, which is already condemned as shaky by his new, scientifically ascertained ideal, and another house, whose construction has begun with the decision that its building (the new theory) must be completed before the old house can be left behind.[2]

The method that should be followed in the construction of the new, scientifically guaranteed dwelling can be summarized in four rules:

1 Do not consider any opinion or statement true, unless you see clearly and distinctly the evidence of it through immediate experience or rigorous deduction (*Evidence!*).

2 Divide every problem into small and simple pieces in order to explain them one by one (*Analysis!*).

3 Begin with the most simple and easy questions and proceed, step by step, to the more complicated ones (*Orderly Deduction!*).

4 Do not omit intermediate problems or steps and assemble the parts of the deduction into a complete whole (*System* and *Totality!*).

It is obvious that Descartes was inspired by modern mathematics, and it is equally obvious that his method has marked the ideal of what now often is called "analytic philosophy" (as if any philosophy were possible without analysis).

As long as the philosopher has not finished his work at the construction's site on the rock, it does not offer him the possibility of being at home in the philosophical realm. In the mean time, he must continue to live a human life, however, just as all who do not care for method and theory. A decent life without philosophical certainty can be lived, if we follow the customs, opinions, and expectations of our surrounding. We conform then to the *ethos* of our time. For Descartes this meant to live as a French *gentilhomme* in Holland, where thinking was relatively free. While his as yet nonexistent (but mentally projected) house is expected to satisfy the most rigorous demands of a scientifically guaranteed construction, the old, philosophically decrepit but still livable, home is ruled by trust in the current beliefs, manners, and traditions of the contemporary culture. In one word it is ruled by the dominant *ethos,* which Descartes finds good enough—not to construct true science, but to support a decent life. However, it is important to note that Descartes counts his Catholic faith and the mores linked to it among the standards that give direction and character to the nonphilosophical part of this philosopher's life.

The scientific ideal that still must be realized has already invalidated the trust on which the old, traditional house was built, but for the time being, as long as one is not an accomplished philosopher, who has finished the new construction according to the new method, one must continue to live in the condemned dwelling. Once the new house is ready, however, the entire life of the true philosopher and of anyone who understands him will be illuminated by the rationally certified truth about human life.

Such truth will be found in the new ethics, crown of the philosophical work to be done. Indeed, Descartes's program for the new construction includes three levels: on the basis of a new metaphysics (first level), a physics must be developed (second level), while the third level has three parts: mechanics, medicine, and ethics. (I translate here into the language of architecture what Descartes allegorizes in the image of a tree of scientific wisdom, which has its roots in metaphysics, its stem in physics, and the three branches that form its crown in mechanics, medicine and the science of morality.) The scientifically warranted ethics will thus occupy the highest level of the house to come. Although the practice of life itself cannot be postponed, we must postpone a scientifically valid justification and guide for it. During the interval between the decision to doubt every opinion and theory and the moment when the new philosophy will have built and insured the new home, we cannot enjoy any certitude about the rational quality of our motivations and behavior, but we do feel the satisfaction of being authentic researchers and being on the way to truth and certified decency.

Descartes seems to have enough trust in the prevailing ethos to consider it the basic standard for resolving existential, and especially moral, problems, at least during the time in which we have not yet acquired the full truth and certainty about ethical behavior. He adopts the existing ethos by stylizing it through "three or four" rules, which he characterizes as forming the outline of a "*morale provisoire,*" a provisional morality or moral code for the interval.

The *first* maxim he adopts states that he will obey the laws and customs of his country. This rule includes loyalty to the religion in which he has been educated. In case of moral controversies or a plurality of probabilities, Descartes decides to follow the most moderate rules, while avoiding all excess, and to side with the most reasonable people among his acquaintances.

Second, he will follow the moral opinions that, despite their lack of certainty, he once and for all will have decided to follow and to consider them sure, safe, and well-established, although they are only probable or even very dubitable. In other words, when life's practice conducts him into a bind between contradictory probabilities, he must resolve it by an act of will that converts an uncertain rule into a surrogate certainty for personal and provisional use.

Third, he decides rather to master his desires for satisfaction than to change the unchangeable order of the world or fate itself, because this is the best way to remain content. The kinship of this rule with the seventeenth-century neostoicism in the style of Seneca and Epictetus is obvious. Despite the bracketing of all past philosophy in the new science, parts of it are apparently good enough to be accepted as normative for life.

The *fourth* rule is even more personal than the third, because it formulates a justification for Descartes's existential decision to dedicate his entire life to the search for philosophical and scientific truth.

These rules and the existential practice they delineate express an emphatic preference for an isolated, conventional, moderate, and intellectually industrious life. In sharp contrast to his concern about the rigorous conditions of his theoretical project, Descartes seems rather confident in accepting a philosophically uncertain moral and religious code as basis for his existential practice. He shows no signs of anxiety about the absence of serious justification for the life he recommends. He even declares that obedience to the first three rules of his provisional ethics suffices for "living as happily as possible,"[3] thus expressing his unproved conviction that *trust* in the existing ethos, if somewhat rationalized, is good and powerful enough for performing a decent, though scientifically un-insured mode of human practice.

Descartes himself never wrote the new ethics he planned, although he gave much sensible advice to princess Elisabeth about virtues and vices, and especially about patience and moderation. Apparently his trust sufficed for conducting a good life, at least as long as the ideal of a rigorously demonstrated ethics was not realized.

Neither did Descartes realize his project of theoretical certainty. Not only did he achieve only fragments of physics and mechanics and hardly anything serious in medicine, but the rock of his metaphysics—*cogito, ergo sum*—has been attacked from all sides and become shaky, and no generally acclaimed mansion has ever been built on it. Neither the exact meaning of thinking (*cogitare,* conscious, self-conscious, intuitive, imaginative, inventive, argumentative, representational, or conceptual thought) nor the status of the ego (the empirical, unconscious, subconscious, self-conscious, transcendental, or phenomenological I) have shown themselves to be obvious enough to obtain unanimous approval. On the contrary, the centuries that separate us from Descartes's philosophical re-beginning have shown a fierce battle about the very idea of a metaphysical foundation and an explosion of more or less interesting but uncertain theories about the right method of thought and science.

Today, after almost four centuries, the variety and divergence of theories, speculations, experiments, and opinions is probably much more pronounced than the philosophical pluralism that convinced Descartes to inaugurate a new departure and procedure for the search of truth. By following Descartes in seeking the remedy for widespread contradiction and uncertainty in the provisional isolation of a scientifically certified philosophy from the ethos that rules the lived, but uncertified parts of human existence, the development of modern philosophy has shown that complete demonstration of highly needed answers to fundamental questions was too high a demand. Few or no rigorous and generally accepted proofs have been given with regard to the most serious questions of human lives. Even purely formal problems of logic and epistemology are not definitively resolved. Plausibility and probability have reclaimed their right—not only in daily life but also in the heart of philosophy. Philosophers have lowered their standards and they have shaped several new traditions and schools, whose foundations, if they laid them at all, cannot be characterized as rocks, but rather as daring theses, more or less inspired views, approximative descriptions, fruitful hypotheses, or revealing perspectives. The republic of philosophers has found more or less skeptical or confident ways to deal with the multiplicity of traditions, perspectives, schools, and leading figures that resists any unification in the name of unshakeable, transparent, and indubitable evidence. After Descartes, even those philosophers who followed his method of clarity, distinction, and scientific analysis have in fact assembled around other versions of a more or less unifying *doxa, ethos,* and *trust* or *faith*—not a religious faith in the narrow sense of a specific religion, but a kind of basic consent and obedience with regard to the enlightened and secular ethos that dominates modernity. Indeed, the modern, secular republic of philosophy shows remarkable parallels with several features of an organized religion. It has its own belief and basic trust, its own manners and customs, authorities, and exemplary scriptures, rules and rituals, manners and customs, symbols and idioms, key problems and dogmas, systems of communication and propaganda, fights and triumphs, forums and judges, accusations and exclusions, prizes, rewards and punishments, celebrations and condemnations, fame, and shame.[4] Who would deny that the various houses, in which differently minded groups of philosophers today seem to be lodged, are ruled by a good deal of trust rather than by the exclusive exercise of demonstrative reason? Perhaps even the ideal of rational demonstration is no longer a shibboleth of philosophical membership.

The new house has not been built, because Descartes's foundation was rediscussed and uprooted without end. Not only was the overall framework of consciousness (or soul) and God given up, but metaphysics as such became a nickname for empty speculation.

The last great thinker who tried to accomplish the construction Descartes had promised was Hegel. After Spinoza, who was the first to accomplish, in his own way, the Cartesian project, Hegel strongly amended the method, on which he then built a gigantic palace—or temple—which he called the *Encyclopedia of the Philosophical Sciences.* He deemed the old house of existential trust superfluous, because he had reused all the good material still found in it, to erect the definitive cathedral of absolute science. However, he understood that the fulfillment of Descartes was not based on the mere evidence of principles and experiments, but on something deeper: deeper than the rationality of a scientific method, but also closer to the faith that Descartes had placed under the protection of his provisional, but existentially necessary, morality.

In both his inaugural addresses of 1816 and 1818 to the students of the universities of Heidelberg and Berlin, Hegel declared that the foundation of philosophy and its only presupposition lies in trust (*Vertrauen*) or faith (*Glaube*):

> In order to begin, I cannot demand anything else than this: that you bring trust to science, *faith in reason, trust and faith in yourself. The courage to truth, faith in the power of the spirit,* is the first condition of *philosophical research;* man ought to honor himself and respect him-

self as worthy to [deal with] the supreme [*sich des Höchsten würdig achten*].[5]

If Hegel is right, the enlightened faith or trust in Reason has replaced, or rather swallowed, the Christian faith that Descartes ranged among the trustworthy but not demonstrably certain tenets of the provisional morality. Hegel's faith was no longer a surrogate for rigorous reason, because it was faith in Reason itself. Reason was the basis of all authentic knowledge, as Descartes had stated, but Hegel recognized that, at least at the beginning of philosophy and science, it is a kind of originary and all-embracing trust that counts, not a singular evidence of the human cogitation about itself.

However, Hegel is the last of the great philosophers who believed that reason could comprehend all trust and make it transparent. Despite the powerful but epigonal currents of Hegelianism, which for a while competed with empiricism and scientism for supremacy in the philosophical republic of the nineteenth century, and a few flare-ups in the twentieth century, the Hegelian cathedral became a historical monument that is visited and admired, but it seems to inspire neither as a guide to existential wisdom nor as definitive completion of the Cartesian project.

Is the project dead? Has skepticism replaced the philosophical ideal of modernity? Perhaps we do not yet possess enough distance to interpret correctly the course that philosophy has taken after Hegel through the revolutions of Marx, Nietzsche, Husserl, Freud, Heidegger, and the great diversity of trends and endeavors that fill its recent history. More than ever we are aware that we cannot point at a stable clubhouse where true philosophers can enjoy a well-concerted cooperation on a joint program, accepted by all and undertaken according to a method without fail. The metaphor of an old and a new house is dead. The past of philosophy has more similarity with a museum than with a house—or even a hotel—and the present shows a confusing crossroads on which many very different travelers are seeking a promising way to the next, more or less enlightening, stage of a search without end. Another metaphor than that of the house—one that

Descartes also uses often in narrating his discovery of the method—might then be more apt to the actual situation: the metaphor of the way (*le chemin*). And instead of trying, just once in your entire life (*semel in vita*), to spend one week of thinking on the metaphysical foundation for a new and perdurable construction, it might be more promising to engage in a long journey suggested by life itself. What encourages and supports us in attempting the as yet unclear and unsure way, is the trust that human life invents its own existential wisdom in going from stage to stage. Such vital wisdom should never be excluded from philosophy, but, on the contrary, be listened to, obeyed, purified, and enjoyed as coming from fuller and deeper sources than the cerebral ones of methodical, perceptive, conceptual, and deductive transparency alone. True method, perception, conceptual grasping, and deductive necessity yield mastery and possession of those realities that allow themselves to be captured and integrated into our rational grids. They condition the ideal of a mastery that converts them into a technological supernature more servile to human use. But won't we miss the more amazing and wonderful, perhaps even more mysterious and divine, parts of reality, if we reduce the entire cosmos to a scientific universe without secrets?

Before I try to answer this question, I would like to sketch—again, only in the barest outline—a pre-Cartesian mode and way (or "method") of approaching the totality of heaven and earth that strongly contrasts with the one I just reflected upon. If we can characterize the philosophical heritage of Descartes's new beginning as an enterprise of methodical destruction and self-conscious construction, supported by an unproved but existentially necessary trust in moral and religious traditions, the approach that I will explore in the next chapter can be characterized as an existentially based trust or faith that tries to discover to what extent the trusted reality can be understood as rationally meaningful: *fides quaerens intellectum.*

SEVEN

Trust in Search of Insight

In chapter 6, we have seen that the Cartesian renewal of science, in its all-encompassing sense, is dominated by *faith* (or *trust*) *in reason.* The reason thus proclaimed to be the sovereign master of truth and certainty can be characterized as the human capacity of conceptual de- and reconstruction. Beginning with the intellectual destruction of all that has been trusted as true and valid, insofar it was not indubitably certain (while continuing to trust the existentially most important part of it in the praxis of one's life), philosophy must produce the certified truth of all that exists by constructing it as a system in which all things are distinguished and linked according to a universal coherence. Hegel, who thought that his system had realized the modern project, at least in its main articulations, concluded that, if any other faith or trust existed outside of the philosopher's faith in reason, the latter would comprehend it as a subordinate dimension of itself. True religion seemed to compete with philosophy in the pursuit of truth, but he spent considerable time and energy on showing that all religions only represented lower-level expressions of the deepest and most complete truth unfolded in the conceptual theory of his philosophy. In his view, Christian faith represents the truth in symbolic forms of the imaginative, narrative, prophetic, and emotional dimensions of civilization; but Reason and philosophy "lift up" that truth from the level of their religious expression to that of conceptual transparency. Trust in reason and philosophy absorbs, and thus elevates or "sublates" religious faith.

FAITH AND BELIEF

There are several reasons why religious faith protests against Hegel's theory. Not primarily because of Hegel's contrast between the conceptual level of human understanding and its prefiguration on the level of affectivity and imagination, but rather because the characteristic intentionality of his philosophy cannot replace the religious intentionality of Jewish, Muslim and Christian, or any other faith. The scientific and the religious intentionality are not two versions of a purely theoretical approach, as if the religious relation could be reduced to another species of the genus *theory.* Faith is not a preconceptual or still unclarified version of conceptual knowledge, but instead a radically different attitude. As *pistis, fides, fiducia,* or radical trust, faith confides the faithful to the God *in* whom they believe. It constitutes a very special variety of being turned toward and attached to God, which—as we have seen—cannot be reduced to an objectifying intention. *Faith* is thus not another word for belief, as if it were equivalent with having opinions, ideas, or explanations about God. The kind of acquaintance involved in faith is related to an attitude that combines longing confidence, complete surrender, receptive devotion, and obedient *ad*oration. The attention of the faithful is captivated by God's invisible facing and wordless protection of their worldly and eternal existence. Their adoration is a responsive movement of opening oneself to the One on whom all things, events, and personal relations depend.

The language (but also the silence) of trust and prayer utterly differs from the language and the silence that express or accompany scholarly interest or simple curiosity. Beliefs and theology speak about God, but prayer speaks to God. If it is true that speaking or writing about God necessarily thematizes or objectifies God, how then is theology, and how are "articles of faith" possible without reducing prayer to examination? Does not an investigation corrupt, or even destroy, the faithful attitude by transforming God into an object that fits the panoramic scene of all theory? If so, God would appear as the summit or as the totality of all objects. But then this superobject would be a finite part of a composite whole or that finite whole itself.[1] Before developing these remarks, let me try to evoke a most naïve, not yet philosophically or theologically stylized, experience of the religious relation itself.

THE RELIGIOUS RELATION

It is extremely difficult to give an accurate description of the appropriate relation that is the core of adoration. However, many descriptions produced by saints and naïve believers can be recognized as genuine evocations, even if none of their descriptions are completely adequate and most of them only metaphorical approximations. At the least, such recognition can be summarized by enumerating a few aspects of trust in God that have not yet been mentioned.

The best descriptions of religious intentionality are found in the core texts of religious naming and celebrating. For a Christian, such texts can be found, for example, in the book of Psalms as read in light of the New Testament, but also in the abundant spiritual and mystical literature of later times that testifies to a history of religious and "mystical" experience. Let me emphasize some of the predicates that such texts present as characteristic for the Christian faith in God.

Attention to God can be compared to an ascending movement of the human heart, because God is high, higher than high, supreme, or rather beyond all height: the Lord who transcends the entire totality of the universe. As such, God's adorable majesty inspires awe, veneration, and profound but trusting fear before the most ancient and ultimate power, which, however, is at the same time experienced as infinitely generous, compassionate, trust-inspiring, loving, and lovable. The infinite distance that separates God from the cosmos and humanity is the most intimate interiority of God's presence in "the soul." Human guilt causes shame and anxiety: "Go away from me!" But anxiety also expresses a most profound desire that drives the faithful toward the God whose forgiving is announced by saints and prophets. Desire, gratitude, trust, adoration, hope, and inner peace conquer anxiety and shame on the way to the One who has been called "the Beloved" and "the Sought" because one falls in love with God when religion becomes an existential reality.[2] Union with the Sought shows itself not only as possible but as hiddenly present in extraordinary experiences that confirm the purest, sublime, yet simple words pronounced or written by experienced seekers. God indeed calls, loves, gives, heals, restores, pardons, purifies, turns, converts, touches, wounds, moves, permeates, inspires, conquers, and consoles.

Concerning the relations between human individuals and communities to God and the role of trust within their ensemble, a few remarks seem useful with regard to the language and the images that are used in religious prayers and liturgies. In the first place we must not only repeat, but also modify what we have said about speaking to and speaking about persons. Even more than do interhuman relations, our relations to God forbid us to change the interlocutor into an object of observation, study, examination, explanation, or theory. If we *must* talk *about* God—and sometimes this might be necessary, for example, in sermons or catechesis—this type of talk should always be subordinated to or marginalized by a prior and ongoing "talking" *to* God. Theology or philosophical discourses about God lose their genuineness when they do not remain intimately linked to celebration, thanksgiving, hope, and praise, because thematization inevitably locates and displays the theme within a broader context or horizon, but God, as being not one among many, infinitely surpasses all finite interlocutors and horizons. This is why Augustine, Anselm, Bonaventure, Thomas, Scotus, and many other premodern theologians begin and end their treatises with a prayer and why they organize these treatises most often as commentaries on psalms, prophecies, and other holy addresses. All talk about God—all kinds of theology, but also all narratives, myths, parables, and explanations—must be written and interpreted as references, commentaries, lateral remarks, or explicative notes in the margin of a prophetic or responsive speaking from one interlocutor to the other.

Second, our audible, silent, or wordless speaking to God is always second: it responds to a prior speaking from or in the name of God. We would not be able to direct our religious attention, if God's attention to us was not first signified by prophets, signs, or an inner voice. Addressing God is always responsive to an earlier speaking that has come to us. It is conditioned by having an inner ear that can be opened or awakened, but also deafened by noise or idle talk. In faith, one trusts that, even if no other human being initiates us to religion, God takes care of this in ways that might be hidden from human understanding.

Third, all our speaking about and much of our speaking to God uses words of a particular language. A wordless speaking to God is possible, but when we call this kind of addressing God "speaking" instead of "lifting our mind (or soul) to God" or something similar, we obviously use metaphors. Now, this sort of language is not strange or ridiculous, because—and this is not a trivial remark, but, in all its obviousness, a radical though often neglected insight—*all* speaking and writing in relation to God is *metaphorical.* In order to evoke the presence of God, who transcends the horizon of the entire universe, we do not have other words, images, concepts, or propositions than those that fit finite realities and possibilities. But God, the Incomparable and Infinite, transcends their realm of fittingness. We do not know how to "infinitize" the meanings of our signs and symbols; we cannot even comprehend what words like *lord, father, mother, wise, compassionate, savior, protector, good, great, powerful, genuine, true, real,* or *strong,* as predicates of "the Beyond," exactly mean, but we know the *direction* into which we must send these words or concepts or images to "reach" and be "received" or "heard" by God.

For metaphors are not static and immobile signs or marks; they reach out and move the users by referring and transferring them to or bringing them up and over (*meta-pherein*) to the infinitely different but still related "dimension" where—we trust—they receive a meaning beyond our comprehension. When we use such metaphors as Lord, Father, or Savior for reaching out to the Incomprehensible and Incomparable, we show that we are not "masters and possessors" of our words and the meanings they should and will receive in reaching their destination, but we testify to our trust that God "hears" and "understands" those metaphors better than we, who hear and understand them in a narrow, weak, and pale sense. In religion, our universe of words and languages becomes one grandiose metaphor of the God who grants these languages and words to humanity for a kind of stammering, called prayer—or, if they are accompanied by commentaries on their (deficient, but well-intentioned) meaning, as tools for God-centered contemplation.

That the metaphorical character of all God-addressing language emphasizes the abyssal, infinite, and incomparable difference of the beyond that separates (and unites![3]) the universe and God is not a new insight, of course, but are we sufficiently fascinated by its hidden meaning and its consequences? Do we, for example, sufficiently understand the dynamic character through which religious metaphors involve us in a movement toward the God whom we want to reach by sending them in that direction? Is this the God "who moves by being loved"?[4] If so, how does He (or She or It, but that difference is also transcended) attract and move? It moves through the human Desire of the Infinite. If this is true, religion is the beginning and end of all human felicity and wisdom.

It is time to return to earth from this flight with medieval theologians to rejoin the company of modern philosophers. Most of these thinkers still saw religion as the normal framework within which human civilization runs its historical course. But the question of how religious faith should relate to the scientific and philosophical endeavors of human autonomy became for them more problematic. Many modern philosophers no longer took for granted that Christian faith could function as a divinely certified basis for their rational exploration of the human universe. I already stated that Hegel's philosophy can be seen as the conclusion of the modern search for a reasonable answer to that question. Instead of inviting his students to an intelligent exploration of a shared religious faith, he asked them to accept another faith: faith in the power of Reason, a power that is able to explain fully the universe of nature and history, including all religious interpretations thereof that have emerged over time.

FAITH AND REASON

In his preface to the *Phenomenology of Spirit,* which is his introduction to the true and absolute *Wissenschaft,* Hegel excludes all edification from scholarly language, but piety and prayer can neither be ignored nor silenced in any phenomenology of the religious dimension. It is clear, however, that the Hegelian brand of reason cannot pray, and certainly not adore, as long as it is exclusively involved in a masterful reconstruction of the universe from the absolute viewpoint of a Subject that, through concepts, propositions, and syllogisms, gathers and comprehends information about the ultimate secret of human existence.

Why is the bulk of contemporary philosophy so silent about God? If it does not like prayer and piety, it still could—and sometimes, for example in its phenomenologies of religion, it should—describe how trust and adoration respond to the God of those who pray. Few scholars show interest, however. Many feel uncomfortable, some of them offer an excuse by saying, "I myself have been educated as a Catholic—or Lutheran or Calvinist—*but. . . .*" However, those philosophers who find trusting God and prayer completely normal and—at least at times—highly enjoyable, are wondering what their colleagues' problem is with religion. They are not impressed by the atheist literature produced by Feuerbach, Marx, Nietzsche, Freud, Sartre, and their kin, because they do not recognize God in the caricatures these authors present and criticize. It is neither difficult, nor a proof of deep insight, to sympathize with accusations against gods or "Gods" who alienate, diminish, suppress, or hurt human freedom, intelligence, love, inspiration, inventiveness, artistic creation, and so on. But which sufficiently educated person would not see that such gods are fabrications of the accusers or bad counterfeits due to inauthentic piety?

Whereas most philosophers of our time exclude God from their field of inquiry or cautiously bracket God's existence (most often, *sine die*), many or most philosophers—from Justin and Clemens to Levinas and Ricoeur (but also including Feuerbach, Nietzsche, Bergson, Husserl, and Heidegger)—were formed as members of a Christian, Jewish, or Muslim community that practiced and liturgically celebrated intimacy with God before they became philosophers. It has also happened, from early on, that some non-Christian philosophers became Christian and continued to exercise their profession, while finding support and inspiration in their new faith for coping with their own and others' existential problems. In both cases, however, Christianity developed its own style of what it, for more than one thousand years, has called *philosophia.*

As the twentieth-century historians of late Greek philosophy have taught us, *philosophia* was the name the Hellenist culture used to characterize a kind of thought that integrated scholarly insights and methods we would call *philosophical* into the meditative practice of a well-formed and well-conducted life: *philosophia* as phronetic and theoretical practice in the service of a well-performed art of life.

It was, of course, inevitable that, during the spreading of the Christian faith, the propagation of this faith would integrate whatever could be used of the philosophy that was produced in the past and present by non-Christian philosophers. Translations of Plato and commentaries on his dialogues, the writings of Cicero and Seneca, Marcus Aurelius and Epictetus, Plotinus, Porphyrius, Proclus, and many more philosophers were transformed into elements of a radically different, and yet recognizably similar *philosophia.* Clemens, Origen, the Capadocians, Ambrose, Augustine, Gregory, and Dionysius are some well-known pioneers of this new tradition. But the name *philosophia* was kept until deep into the twelfth century, although our modern vocabulary forces us to call its style and its products *theological.* It contains too many biblical and typically Christian elements to portray it as philosophical in the modern sense of this predicate; but many of the texts it yielded are conceptually and imaginatively at least as sophisticated as the best philosophy of our century.

The integration and independent elaboration of the philosophical heritage by Christian theologians from Clemens to Cusanus has been characterized by followers of Saint Augustine as a "trust in search of understanding (*fides quaerens intellectum*)."[5] To sketch its style of thought, a brief reminder of its manner or method might be helpful.

Faith in Christ as the central revelation of God was the point of departure for all Christian thinkers, whether they were already acquainted with philosophy or not. The documentation to which they referred as the basis of their trust was the biblical tradition and its communitarian interpretation of the entire human history in light of the life and death of the greatest of all prophets, Jesus the Christ. This "content" of faith needed not only explanation, commentary, and application in ever-changing circumstances but also reformulation of the standard interpretations in other languages and cultural environments than the original ones. The ongoing appropriation of the Christian faith thus was a search for fuller and deeper understanding of its message according to the diversity of available contexts and the possibilities of acquiring as much insight as possible into the revealed—and mysterious—truth in which the faithful put their trust.

Whereas the biblical tradition has elicited this trust by celebrating the God of Abraham, Moses, and Jesus Christ as Creator of the universe, sovereign Lord of history, and Savior of a fallen humanity, pagan philosophers offered metaphysical visions of the cosmos and human nature in light of the *Logos,* the divine, or being as such, while pointing to God as the One on which all beings and ideas depend. In contrast with the metaphorical language of the Biblical storytelling and poetry, Greek philosophy seemed to provide a breath of rationality by transferring many symbolisms onto the level of conceptual insights. This would, for instance, allow for allegorical interpretations of the mystery that was hidden in the revelatory kerygma.

However, the mystery of faith resisted conceptualization, because the core of religion—its addressing and responsive relation—cannot be reduced to theory. As a form of defining or speaking about God, conceptuality misses what it wants to distinguish. *Philosophia* had to accept that God is "greater" than all that can be grasped or mentally possessed, because God transcends all distinctions and comparisons. As Plato already showed, conceptual theory refers to the Beyond in a transferential, and in this sense also metaphorical, mode. It is therefore a mistake to think that the original symbolisms of religious celebration or storytelling can be replaced with a nonmetaphorical—allegorical, scientific, or metaphysical—equivalent.

In the context of faith, conceptuality turns out to be as metaphorical or referring as imaginative, descriptive, narrative, or poetical approaches. By way of illustration, we could, for instance, state that God just as much is and is not a *cause* or *substance* as he is and is not a *rock* or a *father. He* or *She* is neither a He nor a She, neither great nor small, neither (a) being nor nothing, but God is at the same time the most beingly being and the "nothing of all that" in the all-surpassing sense of the absolutely Different.

God does not fit any attempt at comprehension. Theology, like philosophy, falls radically short of establishing God's ongoing presence in history or in the secret depths of the human heart. The only way to express the religious attitude in words is to directly *address* God—and this is always a response—in the mode of a *vocative.*

Examination, analysis, synthesis, vision, and theory cannot fathom God, but adoration in trust, even without any learned explanation, can reach out and arrive where insight does not triumph. Desire and trust reach farther than theory.

TRUST IN GOD

What is the structure of the trust that, in faith, relates Christians to God?

Taking the analysis of entrusting that was sketched in chapter 2 as a point of departure, one must thoroughly modify that analysis to develop an idea of trust as one aspect of the religious relation that is central in this chapter. The following three remarks may indicate the orientation of such a modification.

1. The initiative for entering the religious relation is not taken by the faithful themselves. They have been invited by others to participate in the life and world of a religious community with a long history or they have found themselves participating in it because they were already formed in it.

2. To be part of this community is to trust the kind of life it celebrates as a good response to the God in whom this community puts its most fundamental trust.

3. To trust God is not a mode of entrusting some activity or task to God, as if I were the master of the universe. I am not even my own master although I *am* responsible for my own life, including the faith that has been given to me as mine. I do not have demands with regard to God. I may be angry because of all the disastrous evil for which no humans are responsible and all the evil that is done by them, but, like Job, I must learn to trust that even fate and evil are "in the hands of God" and that they serve a mysterious design thanks to the infinity of the Good.

EIGHT

Trust in God or the Universe?

We cannot live without trust. Even modern philosophers have recognized that the wisdom of life itself and the trust it implies cannot be put in quarantine while they construct their theories—especially not if they attempt to begin with a tabula rasa or a few, almost empty axioms or definitions. But what or who are the realities in which we trust—and cannot but trust—in order to be capable of living humanly?

In chapters 3 to 5, we have rapidly surveyed three constitutive dimensions of the *universe* in which we perform our existence: nature, the society, and the human self. All three include their own history, and the place where they unite is the earth, although a few individuals have begun to explore other globes in space. But is the universe ("the whole" or "the all" as Parmenides called it) all that must be explored to become familiar with the context in which we perform our destiny? Is the universe the first and ultimate, and the overarching reality that justifies a trust without which we cannot live?

Are science or philosophy capable of asking and answering this question? Must religion, or some equivalent like faith, play a role in our exploration?

We need a new start to enter into a dimension that claims to surpass "the all." Is such a claimed beyond possible at all?

EDUCATION IN TRADITIONS OF BASIC TRUST

In the first period of our lives, we trusted, and could not but trust, our parents and early educators. Before my awakening to self-consciousness or reflection, they disciplined my manners and directed my movements, and this did not stop when I showed the first signs of some will or thought of my own. They were the uncontested authorities of my early years, and as such they continue to play an important role in my present life, even if, in the meantime, I have changed considerably. Because my educators, educated by their educators, represented and supported the communities and the traditions to which they belonged, I likewise incorporate those communities' traditions, being myself a player in the same—slowly or sometimes quickly changing—history. I am the product of a past that includes the history of my nation, the traditions of various communities into which I have been introduced, the general culture, and the particular subcultures which have shaped me. However, my participation in the surrounding culture has also emancipated me to some degree: I have been influenced by customs and interests that framed my adult life after I integrated them in a style of my own. What now is characteristic of my life—my character—is the result of several traditions and my personal way of obedience or disobedience toward the ethos that has been imposed on me. Maturity certainly presupposes that I have readjusted what I have received, but even if I have sharply criticized or revolted against my education, I have not been able to autonomously invent my own way of life. Through the incorporation of what I owe to my educators—and indirectly to their educators—I continue to rely on a powerful past. I trust that my having become such as I am contains a trustworthy basis for my own living, even if much of my character still needs overhaul, reform, renewal, and transformation. We trust what we have become, at least insofar as this gives us an opportunity to participate in a mode of existence that is practically inescapable and generally accepted as normal. (Even madness must adjust to a special kind of normalcy for the mad.)

Which fundamental trust does the American culture recommend us to adopt? If we may trust our dollar bills, the answer is clear: "In God we trust." Whether money should be the first place to look for God is not sure, but if even there we meet with God, the nation that thus proclaims its basic trust must be deeply religious. This cannot be said of all Americans, however. After a period during which most Americans saw themselves as Christian, although several of them might have been practical atheists, our epoch accepts all expressions and theories of atheism with as much equanimity or indifference as it shows with regard to Jewish, Christian, or otherwise religious faiths—as long as they do not interfere with public life, which must be regulated in God-less ways.

In academic circles, God is not popular, although some private universities reserve a more or less important place and time for liturgy, religious reflection, and pastoral care to serve those students and employees who consider God relevant for their and others' lives. If, however, millions of people on all social and cultural levels within and without the USA continue to be viscerally involved in religion, it would of course be silly and verging on stupidity to exclude thinking about religion from university teaching and research, even if powerful administrations, unions, or assemblies decided that religious faith and religiously inspired practices were obscurantist or outdated. Even if "trust in God" were only a slogan of uneducated mammonists, it would remain a massive social phenomenon, worthy of serious social, psychological, literary, historical, and philosophical research. *A fortiori* this is the case if many—perhaps most—scholars themselves are involved in a religious form of trust.

In any case, religion cannot be overlooked in a book on trust. Even if, as I noted at the outset of this book, a complete treatise on trust cannot be given here, the relevance of trust within a religious context is too obvious to be silenced. Isn't it in this dimension[1] that answers are sought to the most fundamental question of how we can or should trust the universe in which we exist and acquire some insight into an all-embracing power—Nature? Humanity? History? Thought? Spirit? Life?—that is utterly and definitively trustworthy?

Again, forced by the limitations of my competence and the perspectives with which I am familiar, I must restrict the contours of our subject. From a mostly philosophical, but partly also theological perspective, I will try to elucidate some aspects of the claimed necessity, the meaning, and the relevance of trusting in God, as it is practiced by many well-educated Christians in the context of today's Western civilization. Some readers will see this attempt as outdated; others will demand that all other versions of trust—and especially the Jewish, Muslim, Buddhist, agnostic, and atheist ones—also be presented, but such an encyclopedic project would presuppose the cooperation of many specialists. Even "the" Christian version of trust in God cannot be summarized by one voice, especially not in the actual context of religious crisis and interpretive divergence, which does not leave the Christian community untouched. Thus, I will not attempt to speak in the name of all persons who have convictions and feelings about God and religion—as if any philosopher would ever be able to do this (how many languages should one know and how spacious a heart and head should one have?)—but I hope that some elements of the following text may be recognized as familiar or plausible by its readers, despite inevitable disagreements. As a warning about the perspective from which this chapter is written, I add that the following section is meant to be a tentative fragment about the change of our public culture from a predominantly Christian one to an officially neutral and largely agnostic one.

THE FADING OF RELIGION IN WESTERN CULTURE

A culture has many layers, but all of these layers form a certain unity, although their total composition may show internal contradictions or as yet unresolved tensions between imperfectly absorbed elements.[2] If the characters of certain individuals who belong to a particular culture are marked by serious incoherencies or collisions, this fact may cause problems for their self-trust, forcing them to attempt an internal harmonization. Similar problems become very urgent when a culture, or even an entire civilization, is torn up by internal contradictions. Such a breakdown may happen, even in a rather short time, despite the fact that most signs of normalcy are still in place.

Calling a culture decadent or dying is risky, of course. In general, all cultural diagnoses are difficult. They demand not only a thorough acquaintance with the culture in question, but also a certain distance, and this means that one can look back on its past from a later point in time, which then lacks the immediately lived experience of the past that must be evaluated. However, it is almost inevitable that we consider the hypothesis of an imminent or ongoing breakdown, when a culture, whose most illustrious epochs we admire, no longer represents its ideals in a challenging way that attracts the most promising young adults and adolescents. Is today's general culture, for example, able to trigger passionate dedication among them? Does it convincingly promise future splendor? The details of our diagnosis will be decisive for an evaluation of the trust that underlies the present ethos and the degree of distrust it might suggest.

If a culture is declining, this decline might coincide with the birth of a new era, which, in any case, will save certain elements or aspects of the dying period. The fundamental trust that keeps the community together—and not only the average trust in the still dominant culture of its surroundings—will then undergo a shift, as it is already beset by many doubts and suspicions. Distrust then spreads around, because the foundations are shaken. How deeply people's lives are undermined by distrust depends on the extent to which the normalcy of the accepted traditions is broken. If the transition of one epoch to another is so deep that a fight between two or more cultures already can be described, the key articulations of people's being-in-the-world are undergoing a radical revision. All its components—politics, trade, legislation, business, communication, bureaucracy, art, education, love, gendered relations, and philosophy—are then shifting in ambiguous ways and a variety of possible futures is evoked by the commentators.

A diagnosis of our culture, accompanied by a prognosis of its future, is a project much too grand, even for someone who would master all the required disciplines of sociology, history, cultural analysis, politics, philosophy and so on. As a philosopher who has also studied theology, I must narrow my perspective to a few aspects of our culture, as seen from the perspective of these two disciplines, though primarily from philosophy. But this narrow perspective offers me the possibility of focusing on one basic question: What is the basic, originary, or ultimate reality in which we—as belonging to our still existing but changing culture—might, should, can, or cannot put our fundamental trust? And what is actually happening to this trust and to those who constantly rely on it?

By asking the most basic questions, one enters the dimension of *religion* in a very broad sense of this word, encompassing not only the organized religions, but also all other fundamental attempts at responding—in theory, practice, and affection—to the most radical and serious questions that emerge from human existence as such. As paradigms of religion in this broad sense, I will mention three approaches: Christian faith, with emphasis on its Catholic configuration, Western atheism, and Western agnosticism. The reasons for this selection will become clear, I hope, in the considerations of this chapter.

In chapter 7, we briefly discussed the underlying faith on which Christians rely for their understanding of human existence as a journey toward God, but here I will limit myself to only one aspect of this search: its cultural decline. By *cultural decline* I mean that the cultural expression of this faith (including its relevance and influence) in the public domain of the dominant culture has almost vanished, although relics of it are still lingering. Such a decline is not necessarily identical with disappearance from the private life of most individual citizens, families, schools, associations, clubs of friends, or confessional communities, which may continue to celebrate their liturgies and devotions in nostalgia of the past or expectation of other times.

Indeed, Christianity's vanishing from the public sphere does not necessarily trigger a diminution of its inherent vigor. Christian trust has been and will continue to be very strong in many lives under the most horrible threats and tortures of powerful tyrannies. However, even for many Christians—including for many children of steadfast

Christians who took great care of their childrens' religious education—the biblical stories, the splendor of the "Good News," the liturgical celebration of creation and salvation, the sublimity of mystical poetry, and the highly sophisticated theology of a long, extremely learned tradition have lost their attraction. The *Grand Story* has become pale, in part because of massive ignorance and misunderstanding—even some well-educated intellectuals no longer know what is meant by *trinity, incarnation,* or *immaculate conception*—but also because of the moral, political, and religious scandals caused by ecclesiastical officers and archaic pronouncements issued by some leading authorities.

There are many causes for ignorance. One of them is certainly the suppression of symbolic understanding by a widespread scientistic and technological mindset, but another important cause lies in the inability of many Christians to transmit, in a contemporary language, the greatness of their faith. Sports, music in the park, concert halls, blogging, visits of the Dalai Lama, and so on are found to be more exciting than Christian liturgies, and even abbeys where the grand old liturgy has not yet been replaced with "nice" songs, might present the sacred in long-tested symbols that are too unfamiliar to be enlightening for those who have not enjoyed a thorough education in the historical realities of their faith tradition. Whatever the causes of the massive de-Christianization of the Western world are, the self-presentation of Christian trust has become a pale shadow of the brilliant light it once spread.

Many nuances should amend the statements just pronounced. Fortunately, there are still many holy priests and other saints, good theologians, excellent preachers, and courageous martyrs, but they are not often noticed because of the misbehavior and ignorance of some very visible Church authorities. Moreover, those who practice the most genuine forms of religious devotion are not prone to tout their piety in the public square.

Suspicion, distrust, and aversion regarding Christianity and religions in general have been prepared by the modern emancipation of human freedom from dictatorial and dogmatic powers. We have seen how faith in reason replaced the basic trust in revelation, which once was considered essential for any reasonable discovery of truth. Modern reason showed its own autarchy when the French revolutionaries inaugurated a new calendar and erected the *Temple de la Raison* for the celebration of their new liturgy of Reason. Those festivities did not last, but the nineteenth and twentieth centuries replaced them with a powerful veneration of science and antireligious philosophy, because the old trust in a faith-guided life had changed into the ideal of a wholly rational reordering of nature, society, politics, and history. Those who wanted to defend their religious trust, had to begin by fighting or correcting the widespread prejudice that saw all forms of religion as obscurantism. In order to remain intellectually respectable, one had to justify one's faith before a high court composed of human reason, scientific research, rigorous proofs, and democratic evidence.

Against the backdrop sketched and somewhat sharpened here, all of the following observations are meant to shed some light on one central and final question. Having reflected, in the previous chapters, on the functioning of trust and distrust in particular contexts of human life, we will now ask whether our earthly existence as such also needs a fundamental and all-encompassing trust regarding the whole of humanity and the universe in which it moves. If we cannot live our lives without being animated by a basic and global kind of trust, we must scrutinize the deepest dimension and the ultimate horizon of our human existence as such. To what extent and in which sense can the existentially decisive core of life be identified as the heart of religion? If it can, which role then does, could, or should religion play with regard to the contrast between trust and distrust regarding this world, where good and bad surround us, while encouraging, but also frightening us. Can we enjoy, in hope, the earth in the midst of anxieties?

NAÏVE TRUST AND CRITICAL DISTRUST

If a child is born from parents who are committed to one of the existing religions, it normally learns at a very early stage of its life how to participate in these practices. The prayers and liturgies of one's confession channel one's adherence to the communitarian tradition that has formed one's early religious life. Through worship and personal or familial prayer and practice, a child's life acquires a certain style; it becomes familiar with the climate of a particular religion and gets attuned to a basic disposition or mood. Belief in God's generosity, pardon, and energizing spirit—concretized in eloquent words, practices, and rites—generates trust in the community where this belief is confessed in a credible, inspired, and inspiring way.

A child experiences the way of life it learns from its educators as the right way. Even before many critical questions arise, a basic form of trust installs itself—until doubts from the outside or from within question the religious universe that initially didn't create a problem. Today doubts come earlier than, say, before World War II, but certain forms of dissension or rebellion against dogmatic traditions are as old as religion itself. In the trace of the modern Enlightenment, today's children are emancipated rather quickly; critique of religion is no longer a privilege of heroic or learned iconoclasts.

Numerous children grow up without any form of religious education, however; and many of the initiated leave their confessional ties behind. For many adolescents and adults, religion hardly exists; they seem to feel at home in a climate without religious reminiscences. Still, one cannot say that the question of a basic and ultimate trust or distrust does not regard them, because this question is closely linked to the question of basic and ultimate meaning and its contrary: absurdity or nonsense (or—in an older language—emptiness and vanity). Although the latter question (what is the meaning of my life and the existence of humanity?) is not often debated publicly, no one can avoid asking it in some self-conscious or implicit and half-conscious mode, because the question of ultimate meaning coincides with the question of the longed for *desideratum* that orients the dynamics of human existence. Moreover, this question becomes particularly urgent when we are struck by the inextricable entanglement of sense and nonsense in our world. Can we hope, or even trust, that meaning will win?

How we should approach the question of ultimate meaning is answered in various ways. One way is an overtly religious engagement in kerygmatic and pastoral guidance; another consists in political action or humanitarian activities. One can, of course, also avoid the question itself by embracing a life of having fun, courting partners, getting a job and becoming rich, or—on the contrary—by concentrating on the question, while deciding that prayer or contemplation and generous dedication to the poor are more important than other modes of meaningful praxis.

While asking such questions today, it will be more and more difficult not to get into conversation with Christians, Jews, Muslims, Buddhists, and agnostic or atheist people, who, in their own ways, attempt to find the meaning of "it all." Christians, Jews, and Muslims can probably find agreement in stating that service to all other humans is a decisive test for loving God and that loving God, while being loved by God, is the unsurpassable meaning that should be realized—even—in some hidden way—by those who bracket the question of God or leave it tacit. But how does such love of all humans in God relate to trust in God?

That love of humans does not exclude all forms of distrust is clear: a mother does not stop loving her child when, for example, the child's drug-addiction has convinced her that she can no longer leave it alone with drugs or lots of cash. However, her particular and strictly limited distrust does not entail a loss of the more fundamental trust that her child is not only destined for a better way of life, but also still capable of overcoming the addiction and her distrust.

Love of God, however, excludes distrust, because nothing in God lacks trustworthiness. If God exists, trust is demanded of all who are capable of it. If they have a pure heart, they also will understand that it is abnormal not to love God. But these simple, almost tautological statements do not erase serious riddles and spontaneous lacks of trust. For example: How can there exist so many hateable and untrustworthy realities, if the universe is created by God? And—with regard to the belief mentioned above—why should and how can love of our fellow people coincide with love of God? Not everything in our neighbors is lovable. Whence then does their hateable side come? Why does the human world have certain aspects that I must distrust, if its creator is without any blame?

Losing all belief in God—or never having been a believer, or getting convinced that nothing is more trustworthy and benevolent than human life itself, the world, humanity, or history—does not yet silence the question of what or who would justify a radical and all-encompassing form of trust in our existence, as tied to the universal context in which we are situated. Indeed, the question of meaning itself expresses a most profound need, of which we are always vaguely conscious. When this question becomes explicit in extreme situations, our most passionate desires seem threatened in their very existence. The meaning of our lives seems to become absurd if our need for a basic and life-encompassing trust remains entirely unanswered. Then this need becomes a deadly wound.

IS HAPPINESS POSSIBLE?

St. Augustine summarizes the ancient Greek and Hellenist tradition when he states that all philosophizing is motivated by the desire for *beatitude.*[3] *Beatitudo* is a Latin translation of the Greek *eudaimonia,* which Plato and Aristotle and many other ancient philosophers used to name the perfectly perfect but still human, realization of the supreme *desideratum:* the ultimate well-being, well-doing, well-behaving, and well-feeling of a person who has become exemplary insofar as he or she is beautifully (*eu*) inspired, led, moved, and ensouled by a good spirit or "*daimon.*"[4] It has—alas!—become difficult to evoke what the ancient philosophers mean when they thematized the fact that all humans are driven by a "natural desire" that orients them toward *eudaimonia,* because no contemporary word in English seems to exist for it. In any case *happy* and *happiness* are much too worn out, while *bliss* likewise hides the essential goodness of the most beloved and longed for ideal of being human behind the name of a dazzling experience.

In chapter 4 I argued that all our activities are indeed driven by a fundamental desire to accomplish our personal destiny in a way that deserves the greatest possible joy, gratitude, and admiration. Not only philosophers from Plato to our days, but also the wise of all great civilizations and the prophets of the great religions have concentrated their pathos on that target. But are we capable of realizing their ideals?

May we hope to be successful in becoming the persons we are meant to be? Is it not only possible but also sufficient to trust (in) our own talents for realizing goodness, beauty, and existential perfection? Or do we need and must we trust in other forces that do not fall under our own command: benevolent people and institutions, auspicious events, angels, gods, or half-gods? In other words: Which conditions must be fulfilled, besides our own efforts, to make the overall success—beatitude—of our human lives possible? Can we trust that the world and our existence in it are such that we may hope for a final result that proves to be the desired end?

How often have we met with people who already seem to have become happy in the full sense briefly indicated above? Apparently a perfect realization of one's destiny is difficult. We are no exceptions, if we perceive ourselves as still failing in living splendidly; and an hour of world news suffices to rouse horror of the massive misery, injustice, violation, and perversion of human existence in all parts of the world. The multiplicity of murders, lies, distortions, acts of hatred and betrayal, together with our own unhappy experiences, are depressing. Aren't they sufficient to kill all naïve inclinations to investing our trust into the real world of which we are a part? But if despair or distrust wins on the basic level of existence, how can we then still pursue our personal happiness otherwise than by complete isolation—which, of course, is neither happy nor possible?

One could answer the disillusioned by remarking that the media-driven display of suffering and crime, coupled with our personal experiences of injustice and malevolence, offer a caricature of the world, and that, in fact, most people are still rather decent and moderately happy persons, who also contribute to the social well-being of their surroundings. But numerous obstacles against the possibility of existential success seem unconquerable. So many individual and communal failures are obvious to those who are not morally blind, that discouragement or cynicism remains a constant temptation. Even together, we cannot radically change the disastrous parts of our history nor the cruel outbursts of a rather unmotherly nature, which often enough loses its temper.

Against a systematic enumeration of all the disasters that dissuade us from trusting the world in which we live, one may object that such an appraisal can only yield a one-sided lamentation but not a balanced judgment about the right proportion of trust and distrust that is deserved by today's state of humanity. Before we make up our balance, we must at least form an approximative idea of the cosmic and historical mixture of good and bad that frames and permeates our embodied souls.

But who can conquer the required perspective for such a universal overview and how can we describe it from there without exaggerations or omissions? Both the splendor and the horror of human existence must be painted in all its glorious and distressing aspects, but who is able to escape the partiality of individual experiences and other contingencies like the recent or already forgotten events that have shocked or joyfully impressed our historical memory? And which score of good and bad delivers a satisfactory result? Doesn't our goal—beatitude, bliss—exclude *all* evil?

At this point, we must ask whether we are really interested in an exact score (at which time?) of the fight between good and bad. If it is true that the only fully trustworthy result of a perfectly meaningful outcome consists in the personal and collective perfection of humanity, would this perfection—a truly and fully good universe—then not already be undone by one irreparable disaster? In other words, would existence as such not deserve a conclusive distrust as soon as it is clear that it finally will run into a form of destruction, unhappiness, lack of meaning, or nonsense? But even if my personal history or world history as a whole does not end with total destruction, but only realizes more bad than good, wouldn't a generalized distrust be more recommendable than any basic and overall trust?

GOOD AND EVIL

In the abundantly rich countries of the Western hemisphere, most middle-class people live comfortable lives, while trying to ignore the scandalous contrast between the great number of luckless people in their own surroundings and even more so in the rest of the world, on one side, and a very small number of outrageously ultrawealthy people, who have only immaterial and some health problems, on the other. The ways in which the question of trust versus distrust assails different people cannot be answered by one answer for all. However, in a very generalized sense, we may venture to state that everyone who is not seriously tempted by suicide holds on to a certain degree of trust in the normal functioning of the universe. The surprising regularity and beauty of nature in all its dimensions and details, as studied by the sciences and celebrated by the poets, is striking. The stratification of our society, together with its traditional mores and cultural heritage, creates an atmosphere of security, which makes us feel at home in this world, despite scandals and disasters, which, in the end, remain exceptional.

A treatise on the existence of a widespread basic trust could begin with an impressive list of all the conditions that silently canalize the course of human existence in a familiar universe. The description of this universe would involve an endless stream of phenomenological, scientific, and philosophical stories and analyses of its forever unfinished history of splendid exploits in politics, science, philosophy, art, and religion. Its admirable regularity and all other forms of orderly arrangement arouse trust: We know what to expect and how to react. We are settled and at home. The world is marvelous and hospitable—a wonder!

But nature and history, even humanity as a whole, are also terrifying! Yes, but that aspect—the horror—is due to the exceptions and irregularities that disrupt their normalcy. Still, a complete list of such "exceptions" is long, perhaps *too* long, especially if we do not restrict it to the outbursts of an untamed nature, such as volcanic eruptions or unpredictable tsunamis, but also admit the human-made disasters to our list, such as the wars that never seem to end, the pollution of soil, water and air, the economic calamities, and huge political malfeasance.

There are periods in which the "exceptions" are so huge and numerous that many people begin to perceive them as a disastrous replacement of the trusted rules with a kind of normalized abnormalcy. The established order seems to vacillate, fate becomes volatile, our lives lose certainty, guidance, and outer as well as inner peace. The world is no longer a miracle of trustworthiness; we can no longer count on it. The universe has become a mixture of marvels and hostility. If such a perception spreads in a culture, it will be visible and audible in its art—especially in poetry, novels, paintings, and music. Often such a change signifies the decline of an epoch that has had its time. And this is—I believe—the case for us when we look back on the last centuries.

Much of the literary, pictorial, dramatic, and musical art, produced in the first and second half of the twentieth century expresses fragmentation, anxiety, distress, skepsis, and despair; but after the all too numerous wars—civil, colonial, anticolonial, imperialist, and anti-imperialist—and many natural or manmade disasters, the West seems to have returned to the disenchanted, but somewhat less pretentious, conviction that the world goes on as it went before. Even during the cruelest years of the cruelest dominations, many people escaped the cruelest practices and those who survived are prone to forget the threats that formerly undermined the very possibility of living itself. Even in the very direst of all circumstances—the Gulags and ethnic cleansings—most people find still reasons for maintaining a minimum of trust. Clinging to life, despite extreme oppression, always includes some remainder. It is not easy—because it would kill all meaning—to annul completely the perspective of a possible, hopefully better future. Apparently, the life already lived and provisionally saved has revealed too much good to give up all desire and hope of survival.

Would it be true that all of us are supported by a very deep and indestructible trust more tenacious than all anguish and despair? Let us try an imaginative experiment by weighing how, in an average person, an average balance emerges between good and bad experiences—and therewith a balance of the trust- or untrustworthiness of future chances. Despite the large differences between lucky and unlucky persons, it seems possible to perform such an experiment by way of a comparison between the glorious and the terrible aspects of human existence in this world of our time. On the one hand, we must then consider to what extent it is great to exist and how the overall experience of this greatness elicits trust in a further development of the existence we enjoy in growth, education, being nursed, respected, and loved, and in playing a role during fortunate events and interpersonal experiences. On the other, we must try to measure the depth and the extent of the existential burden that accompanies most or all mortal lives: all sorts of sickness, violence, pain, cruelty, suffering, abandonment, loneliness, death, murder, betrayal, hypocrisy, and lies, lies, lies—in brief: *death, evil, guilt, suffering.*

DEATH

To begin with, *death* surely seems a strong objection against the possibility of human happiness: How could a mortal being ever be or become happy? Isn't the desire to maintain a happy situation forever against all destruction an essential part of our deepest drive? How then could the imminence of dying coexist with the realization of a blissful *eudaimonia*?

Even before we can try to answer this objection, we must ask to what extent we are able to reflect at all about death. Are a description and conception of death and dying possible at all? No individual can speak about his or her own encounter with death, because we come always too early for that event. We do speak about the deaths of others, but we do not have any shared experience of their dying. What can we say about it? What else than that its very experience escapes us, because it remains a secret of those who left us by experiencing it? Whatever empirical evidence about someone's dying is available, death itself is shrouded in mystery. It generates wordless awe but silences all commentary.

There is something strange in our knowledge about our own mortality. The standard pattern of definable knowledge focuses on phenomena that are confined to a certain context or horizon. In order to describe a phenomenon, we must determine how it distinguishes itself from its context, while maintaining certain relations with it. Insofar as it "presents" itself, someone's dying happens in a specific space and time, where it takes (a particular) place. One strange aspect of my death, as an "event" that I will undergo, lies in its escaping from my existential temporality: the fact of my dying, as an "encounter" with death, is an event that has a before (the past of my life, which then comes to an end), but it does not have an after, because death destroys the very possibility of my still "having time." What remains, when I die? In any case not the living human being I will have been until death replaces it with something entirely different: a corpse. Since a corpse has little to do with *me* (can it speak or signify as an "I"?), I am no longer there or then. I have passed and if "I" *am* still somehow, this "I" can only *be* or *exist* in an invisible, unhearable, unsmellable, untouchable, unspatial, atemporal, and unseizable mode. Aristotle already understood that the mutation of a living individual into a corpse (or—if that is possible—into the twofold existence of a soul and a corpse) constitutes what he calls a *substantial* (or essential) change.

If my death let me vanish from the space-time that continues insofar as it contextualizes the living, my own mortality cannot be present as an object or "normal" phenomenon. Those who surround me before, during, or after my "departure" can stare at the ending of my last expressions or at the relics that replace my presence; but they can only vaguely and irreally imagine—not know—what dying for the dying is. For them, there is still time to discover what my "going away" for them means, but for knowledge about their own dying they must wait until they themselves may experience how death cuts their life's line, which from that moment on no longer fits the laws of space and time.

If it is true that human knowledge needs space and time to be "objective," this necessity might explain why thinking about our own death is so difficult and unreal. It might also explain why experiencing and thinking about the dying of others is so radically different in view, tone, and emotional resonance. However, instead of pursuing here the project of a complete phenomenology of death, we must return to the question of how human mortality may inspire trust or distrust in response to human existence as such. To answer this question, we should not isolate our death from the rest of our lives. Whereas we, as children, counted on others for taking care of our basic protection and correction, once adult, we know how to deal with people, things, and institutions. But obstacles and competing forces offer resistance or threaten to undo what we have realized. Our own energy and skills dwindle and the end of "it all" is absence—except that perhaps some powerless name or fame lingers awhile before we are forgotten.

What does this end mean for those who have died? Very few of them remain present through others' remembrance of their past as educators, heroes, composers, or examples of generosity, but none of such remembrance breathes new life into the dust they left behind. Their struggle for happiness is over, just as our struggle soon will be over. But what, in hindsight, is the result of their and our struggling? When did they and when will we, if ever, accomplish the happy fulfillment or the conclusive meaning of the destinies that were assigned to us?

If it is possible to reach and accomplish a certain degree of happiness or perfection in some phase of human life, the fact of losing or destroying it—and what is a more certain loss than death?—must be a real disaster. But never having reached a restricted period of fulfillment or relative happiness seems worse. Are all dead then ultimately unhappy? Is it inevitable to fail precisely in that aim which we desire most of all to accomplish? Are we obsessed by a success that cannot be conquered but only continually delayed and then destroyed? Is life in the end and from the beginning condemned to failure?

Are we too demanding? Since we are no gods, only *hubris* can expect to be capable of producing perfect and everlasting happiness. Be content with an incomplete, imperfect, never fully successful unfolding! Such imperfect happiness is not without meaning, to a certain degree even good and beautiful. It may inspire others to appreciate your work and follow your example. The desire that drives us may be immoderate, but its exaggeration might generate some temporal splendor that deserves admiration, even if it is accompanied by nostalgic resignation about the brevity of its shining.

Although death puts an end to all success, its sealing off of my life makes me sharply aware of this life as a whole and of my responsibility for its overall meaning. In the best case, this meaning will be restricted to a limited time of bliss, but is that not enough for the mortals we are? Doesn't death also save us from much sadness, because of the pain and shame that go with a long senescence, especially in an epoch where lengthening debilitated lives without end is promoted by well-intentioned or greedy bystanders?

An ethics of dying and preparing yourself for death is needed: Be modest by not demanding too much time and health; do not overstep the proportions that are given to you! Learn that a singular life is only this: a phase between the miracle of being born and growing up for a single role in a collective drama with the chance of performing well, sometimes even beautifully, in order to finish worthily. *Carpe diem* and *mēden agan.*

Between enthusiasm about one's chances and anxiety in the face of various threats and dangers, a mixture of trust and distrust—every so often revisable—accompanies human existence, if it sees itself confined to a relatively short performance of its destiny. However, the resignation indicated here presupposes that one can give up the love of perfection and overcome the idea that the real *Desideratum is infinite and eternal.* It thus would exclude all forms of immortality, including the idea of an incorporeal survival of the soul as well as the Christian faith in an immortal union of the incarnated self with the infinite life of God. But are such forms of hope trustworthy or are they rather phantasmatic expressions of a narcissistic obsession? Survival after death is certainly an amazing idea, which many people have deemed profoundly edifying, but improbable, while others call it incredibly presumptuous. But millions believe in an eternal destination and live their lives in light of it.

If any union with God is impossible, then also the infinity of human Desire must be an illusion or a lie, and more limited possibilities of hope must be considered to be the result of a well-lived life. Our radical orientation should then be understood as a more restricted one; for example, as a merely historical way of still being remembered and influential in the words and actions of one's children, pupils, readers, followers, or admirers. Whatever the true *Desired and Beloved* is, the question of hope and trust does not go away, even if we constantly delay it until we already are on the verge of death. As long as we do not discover a trustworthy answer, we practice a sort of trust without name or hope—unless we give up the search before a credible promise convinces us that our Desire indeed wants more than "it all" and *cannot* disappoint us radically.

If death is nothing else than the summit of destruction, insofar as each of us is concerned, should we not single it out as the worst disaster that befalls all individual lives? Further on I will argue that this is not the case, even from a not-explicitly religious standpoint, because meaninglessness, absurdity, and especially hatred of meaning and dignity are worse. But being reduced to dust is certainly an extreme misfortune—unless, as many or most cultures have thought, death is a most startling transition to a transformed kind of existence, in which the core identity of the dead is preserved, perhaps even in a more fortunate mode than the former, mortal one.

In our time, when relatively few intellectuals expect truth or wisdom from myths or other evocations of a heavenly life, many—and among them famous philosophers—insist exclusively on the definitive character of dying once and forever. According to Martin Heidegger, for example, death is a confrontation with the nothingness that marks all the phases and details of human existence as condemned to disappearance.[5] All or some of the remaining works of the dead may still be relevant, but the persons who produced them "are" no longer "there." There are, however, others who may reproduce or transform their works into new performances of limited meaning.

This is not the place to summarize the long history of attempts at preaching or imagining an ongoing life after death, but today's widespread skepticism is not a refutation of the Desire for eternal life that animates those who accept the answers of various confessions. Survival should not be separated from the human striving for meaning. Medical and dietary practices have already lengthened the average age, but if many lives have paid for their lengthening by a vilification of their meaning, one cannot call such survival a progress with regard to a more meaningful but shorter life. The potential hero, who delays his death in exchange for a later but shameful death, is contemptible. The death of a short but glorious life that reached the highest possible form of union with the infinite is certainly preferable to an extraordinarily long but mediocre life. And what about the trustworthiness of such lives?

If meaning—not length—is the measure for celebrating a good life, death is less dangerous than missing the chance of becoming as good as one can be. Consequently, the *Angst* evoked in us by our own mortality is not the deepest dread that can assail us. A much deeper anguish grips us when we are frightened by the threat of living in vain or badly. But what is "living well"?

The answer to this radical but absolutely universal question, which every singular person has to answer in some way, cannot depend, we trust, on the acquisition of a professorship in philosophy. The real answer is given in that core of each one's singular self-awareness, which has been called a guiding voice or *conscience.* Conscience is neither a kind of science nor a noisy voice, but rather the silent and most intimate, extremely serious and decisive affection that orients and drives each one in a strictly personal way toward a strictly personal manner of existing, although it has much in common with the "vocation," and the goodness or "perfection" of all other singular persons. *Destiny* is another name for the destination indicated by that voice. Instead of the *sense* or *meaning* I have to realize, we can speak of my destiny as that which—or rather the one who—I am meant to be, and therefore to become. The impersonal mode of "being meant" fits our experience well, insofar as your or my destiny is not left to your or my choice, although a limited possibility of personal deliberation and decision participates in the unrolling of each one's individual, but heavily contextualized and omnimodally determined, existence.

Freedom is a reality, but it is not primarily a power of choice, it does not create its own conditioning, and it is decisive for the way one embraces or modifies the suggestions that are revealed by each singular destiny over the course of its own more or less authentic realization. The deepest anguish that assails the human heart is the fear of having lost the right direction, of being at a loss in orientation, of not becoming what the entrusted life is meant to be. Death is horrible if it kills me at a moment in which it is no longer a vague threat, but instead the unveiling of a caricature: this—a lovable father, friend, guide, saint—you could have been, but look at these distortions! Death loses, however, much of its terror if it appears as the conclusion of a well-performed life, exemplary in its dedication to its own vocation. Wouldn't such a life be even infinitely more splendid if sustained coincidence with its originary meaning has made it immune against destruction? That would be a truly triumphant response to the somber observation, mentioned above, that the destructive end of a perfect life is a most disappointing outcome of its exemplarity.

In all times prophets and thinkers have searched for an answer to our desire for a happy survival. Some have argued or testified that the human spirit survives the destruction of the corporeal element it animates, but others have dared to affirm that the human person as such (including the person's essential corporeality) lives eternally. What grounds can one present for such a startling—though exhilarating—belief? If this belief is wholly unfounded, must we then not return to some superstitious, godless and God-less or Stoic myth or to austere but disappointing forms of resignation? If so, what sort of trust could the certainty of death still inspire?

EVIL

Worse than death—and a deeper reason for distrust—is the devastating omnipresence of evil in our world. Would a complete description of all evils that spoil the splendor of nature and history only contest the description of all that is good in it or even be more overwhelming? In any case, neither the experience nor the identification of any evil can be separated from the good that is wronged by it. Evil cannot exist or be thought on its own, because it is a perversion of some good that thereby is bereft of one or more good elements. This axiom is common to the biblical tradition, which came to us through the Jews, and to the philosophical tradition that we inherited from the Greeks.[6]

The two myths that together form the beginning of the Bible form a diptych. Whereas the myth of creation (Genesis 1:1–2:4) celebrates the entire creation as immediately depending on God's word and consequently as completely "good" (1:4, 10, 12, 18, 21, 25) and "very good" (1:31), the second myth (Genesis 2:5–3:21) tells us that it is the human race (Adam), as seduced by a devastating but very obscure kind of temptation, which causes all originarily good and beautiful realities to be tainted and partially hostile, without, however, losing some fundamental goodness and trustworthiness.

Ancient Greece also had its myths about the origins of good and evil. Its epics and tragedies tell us how heroic glory is brought down by fatal hubris, whereas its philosophers attempted to resolve the riddle of evil as an enigmatic "lack of being," because being as being can only be good. This is not the place to retrieve their metaphysics of evil, but if we may follow the guideline formulated above, we will continue a very long tradition according to which all evil is secondary: a caricature or forgery, never genuine, originary, or originated by the Origin.

A second precision is necessary before I mention some of the main figures in which evil reveals itself. To avoid muddles, I will begin by making a distinction between all kinds of evil that are attributable to free agents, such as well-deliberated murders, and evil that befalls us without being caused or motivated by any will, such as an unexpected volcanic eruption that destroys an entire village. Even if this distinction might get blurred in the course of further reflection, we need it for a provisional clarification of our question about trust or distrust with regard to the roles of the world and humanity itself in the causation of various evils.

Many forms of destruction and deficiency that harm our bodies, are not due to any human will. They belong to the natural course of all corporeal life, although we remain amazed by their inexorable, yet often unpredictable, character. That most of us cannot escape such suffering, although we do not know why this is the case and why the different proportions between the victims are as they are, is an enigma. Very often, there is no answer to our asking "Why?!" "Why them?!" "Why me?!" If the answer were that someone had decided to make us pay or atone for some mischief, we would at least have a reason and an interlocutor, whom we could, like Job, summon to explain his or her intent. But can we experience groundless suffering as anything other than a form of arbitrary and unjustified terror? How could we trust any universe or god who would like to subject us to such terror? Other forms of suffering, such as the distress that enemies, secret services, heads of states, financial moguls, petty criminals, or disloyal friends might cause, are to some extent easier to understand than anonymous disasters. When I face an enemy, I am still involved in a personal confrontation for which reasons can be found. Facing the torturer is my last defense. But very often I am not facing any person, because I am crushed by an anonymous power or caught in a system that makes me complicit with its murderous effects. That I "must" suffer, seems then not only unfair, but completely irrational.

A full description of the mixed world in which we are involved would give a picture of its main dimensions and levels from the perspective of its glory as—alas!—tainted and distorted by perversions. Such a description would change with the historical twists and turns that occur—evil, too, has a history—but striking similarities between the style of the good and the bad sides of each epoch would show its underlying character, which has its own profoundly tragic aspects.

Some of the most glaring forms of evil are found in today's combination of ruthless capitalism with imperialism, economic colonialism, ecological irresponsibility, and international pollution of air, water, soil and light. The accumulation of outrageous wealth keeps the poor impoverished. Dictatorial and pseudodemocratic states and an almost omnipresent corruption create a climate of blackmail and exploitation. Greed and power flourish, despite the solidarity of activists, who sometimes imitate the terrorist tactics of contemporary warfare between nations. Ethnic cleansing, extermination camps, indiscriminate bombing, organized raping, systematic torture, and unbridled falsification get rid of honor, honesty, and human dignity. Injustice finds its ways into mistrials and forced or buyable elections. Consolation is sought in narcotics, guns are everywhere, the prisons are overfull, and work is a difficult-to-acquire commodity. Loyalty among friends, spouses, and families becomes rare; the general climate favors suspicion and mistrust. Who, in such a world, is able to remain decent, friendly, reliable, authentic, sincere?

The list of justified lamentations can be augmented with a list of similar perversions on the levels of conversation, the media, entertainment, music, photography, theater, and other arts. Even science and philosophy are not exempt from malignity. Quite a number of scientists have been employed as willing servants of antihuman regimes and it is no secret that certain mass murders—such as the nuclear erasure of Hiroshima and Nagasaki—have never been regretted by the nation that performed them. It is, of course, true that well-performed science as such does not lead to moral or immoral decisions; but can we, in the actual situation, trust that all scientists will resist the temptation to sell their discoveries to powerful institutions or associations that offer billions for the execution of murderous contracts?

Moreover, we certainly must not forget the humbug that is promoted and the scandalous betrayals perpetrated by some bureaucrats of venerable religions. If those whose task consists in supporting our quest for ultimate meaning fall prey to lying and impenitent self-justification, who or what could then still be a rock of trustworthiness?

GUILT

As infants, we were naïve. Although birth, as being exiled from a nurturing womb into a dreadful world, must have been a frightening shock, we could rely on those who saved us from dying. We were not yet aware of all the threats that would endanger our growing up, but soon we would discover that the human context, far from being a paradise, is ravaged by suffering, inexorable death, corruption, and other kinds of evil, and that we already played a part in the organized egoism of greed and negotiations about being honest or dishonest.

Some participation in ongoing evils we cannot avoid. Buying the bread and the milk we consume implies support for the rapacious capitalism that dominates the unavoidable economy. Using cars and planes has us comply with the violence and corruption that is committed in the name of sacred oil. And so on. But let us not forge alibis by accusing only anonymous entities. Sincerity demands confession of our own private and public lies and injustices, even if these confessions undermine our own and others' trust in our trustworthiness. Death destroys life, but if the meaning of life is to be good in becoming good, evil is an attack on its meaning. Since we are not without failures, we recognize that we, like so many others, are accumulating guilt. I myself participate in resistance to the good and its life-giving generosity.

In some of the preceding chapters, I have pointed at the distrust that evil in some of its natural and historical manifestations deserves. While reflecting on self-trust, I could not ignore the failures through which I undermine all claims to innocence with respect to the meaning of my actions and intentions. From the perspective of the present chapter, our personal and common guilt is even more disquieting because the perversion of genuine meaning and decency is much worse than the inevitability of dying. It is possible to make peace with death, or even to welcome it, but insincerity, corruption, and perversion deserve only hatred and distrust.

Perhaps it is possible to sincerely reflect on one's own and others' pasts without feeling sadness, shame, regret, and remorse about those events and experiences in which we more or less willingly participated in evil's obstructions. Perhaps it is even possible to represent human history as an unstoppable progress in triumph after triumph of Reason and Success, without paying much attention to the dark events that happened in the margin as "collateral damage." Others, however, might think that such presentations of the human history testify to crass ignorance, outrageous naïveté or stubborn thoughtlessness. But whatever story one tells, a frank recognition of our own ongoing participation in evil's hideousness is necessary. It is, however, so painful that denials of guilt, though hardly forgivable, are understandable.

At least two enormous questions emerge from the facts: How can we trust this world and our entanglement in it? How can we—how can I—trust that there is a way of being liberated from guilt? Is there any possibility of becoming innocent again? Pardon, *katharsis,* purification, rebirth? These questions are asked in all religions and in some—but very few—philosophies. Why don't they take the forefront of our thinking about Desire and Trust?

Guilt and death are often associated, and this is understandable, because death puts its final seal on a life that only then is ready for an overall evaluation. Moreover, even after conversion and purification, it seems almost impossible to stop altogether one's participation in the worldwide mixture of injustice and disrespect. Should death be welcomed because dying seems to be the only way of escaping further culpability?

SUFFERING

The world is not a paradise. In all probability it will never become nor has it ever been one. History—the history of the last four centuries no less than that of older times—has sufficiently demonstrated that humanity never escapes its destiny of failing, committing crimes, suffering, and regretting the disasters by which it is ravaged with or without its own cooperation. Since birth, or even before, we are harmed by enemies, the difficulties of social life and the political, religious, and cultural entanglements in which we are involved. Many of us suffer from systematic greed and exploitation, wealthy and petty thieves, hateful killers, and envious rivals, but also by our own stupidity and corrupt affections and by disasters of the surrounding nature.[7]

A complete phenomenology of human suffering would sketch how many varieties of suffering ravage our world. Human existence would be so much more enjoyable if it were not tainted by innumerable forms of pain, sickness, humiliation, loss, hatred, war, and persecution. A complete map of suffering would silence those who cannot stop praising the glory of the earth and its inhabitants, their social institutions, and the history of humanity. If we are sincere, we recognize that the world's splendor is corrupted by overwhelming experiences of horror.

From the perspective of trust, the history of suffering is experienced as a scandal. If we cannot count on a reasonably enjoyable way of life, because the "natural" and normal processes that rule our situation are so often spoiled by widespread suffering of body, mind, spirit, and dignity, don't we then live in constant fear and anxiety? Who could ever become happy or lovingly embrace human existence under those circumstances? Radio, television, and the web inundate us every day and every hour with bad news about the misery and murderous cruelty that victimize millions of our young and older brothers and sisters. Natural disasters, dictatorial politics and ruthless capitalism reduce them to extreme poverty and slavery, while civil and other wars ravage many nations at the same time or one after the other. If we, once in awhile, are not too preoccupied by our own problems to consider the state of our world as a whole, it is difficult not to be incensed about the unhappiness that almost constantly threatens its basic order and generosity. What has happened to us? What have we done with the goods of our earth? Much harm is certainly due to our own mismanagement, but much harm is also being done by natural powers that we have not been able to tame. Why is nature, besides being a mother, also an enemy? Or why are the gods of nature angry at us? And why is our own history so violent and destructive?

We might still have a vague feeling that all suffering is somehow connected with human guilt—a feeling that seems expressed in the myth of humanity's ("Adam's") fall into sin,[8] but few modern philosophers have insisted on a fundamental connection between human evil and human misery. Neither sin or guilt, nor suffering as such have been abundantly analyzed. The framework was dominated by illusions about Enlightenment and scientific, moral, political, and technical progress. The classics from Plato to Kant, on the contrary, paid much attention to the many obstacles that separate us from happiness, which was primarily understood as a virtuous, and only secondarily as an enjoyable or agreeable way of life; but even they, except perhaps the Stoics, did not indulge in extended analyses of pain or misery.

Today, however, we seem to be more depressed and obsessed by pains, handicaps, and other, especially corporeal and psychical, forms of harm than by moral evil or spiritual deficiencies. Has Western civilization relegated its traditional focus on moral amelioration to priests and preachers, while reserving its intellectual concentration on medication and other techniques of corporeal prevention? If this is indeed the case, do we know anything about the reason(s) for this shift?

One could begin with the remark that the kind of suffering that gets much (the most?) attention is indeed the most obvious, external, and corporeal one. Is it possible to surmise that a materialist and more scientific than philosophical ethos is more interested in the contrast between health and handicaps or between comfort and displeasure than in the inner struggle of "the soul" between moral imperfection and the acquisition of a better "state of mind"? Such a preference for visible and clearly demonstrable "states" over internal dispositions fits well into the preferred style of today's communication: everything must be observed, visualized, shown and captured in pictures or images—not by means of mythical narratives or rites, but in exact reproductions of obvious and "unfakeable" facts. Inner peace and anxiety or love and contempt, however, are not as controllable as wounds or organic defects.

Even if this remark is not pertinent to the present question, it seems phenomenologically correct to state that suffering, as immediate confrontation with a harmful, oppressive, depressing, or humiliating deed or event, occupies and retains the attention of most people with a more intense and continuous force than the experience of having committed some form of moral evil. The pain of remorse, for example, can be felt deeply, but if the deed by which it is caused is not too horrendous, the remorse can wear out or find some accommodation with better memories of the actor's guilty conscience, whereas a serious and obvious wound or sickness seldom stops capturing the victim's attention. The immediacy with which such a corporeal harm besets me, does not permit me to bypass or ignore the pain. It occupies my feeling, which resists, repels, and rejects it while not being able to do this effectively. I am thus in a bind, divided in two parts that cannot be reconciled.

Whatever the case, certainly those forms of suffering that befall someone without being caused by the victim or any other human perpetrator—such as a volcanic eruption—attract the most attention and resistance. What makes such kinds of suffering a scandal is primarily the experience of its apparently unjustified or irrational character. A spontaneous, almost inevitable, response to it is then very often: Why does this occur to me? Did I *deserve* this? No, there is no good moral reason for subjecting me to this abominable event. What hits me is an injustice. If so, however, who or what committed this injustice, if it is neither the victim nor any other person? The only other possibility seems to be that the harm is done by an impersonal entity, such as a volcano, a river, a sea, a thunderbolt, an animal, or—in general—nature. But if nature is created, are the gods or is the Creator then not responsible for this injustice? Or am I so blind that I have not even noticed my own or others' involvement in the cause of my misfortune?

Some philosophers might introduce here anonymous, but still human, culprits, such as an unjust social system or traditions of discrimination that make victims, although such systems and traditions cannot be identified with particular individuals whom we could hold responsible for the evil that hits the suffering subjects. But then the similarity of such anonymous forces to natural forms of causation could prompt us to ask why the God of the universe, which is as much social and historical as natural, should not be seen as responsible or coresponsible for its disastrous effects. Is the Creator of the universe, who also leads its history, unable or unwilling to prevent evil and suffering from spoiling this universe?

From the fact that our universe is not just rotten or all bad, but an ambiguous mixture of good and bad factors, a radical *aporia* emerges for both believers and God- or godless thinkers. For the latter, the question is, of course, how can one explain the actual existence of a reasonably and basically good cosmos and humanity, and why has this universe, if it was originally good, become a mixture of good and bad things and events? Those who put their trust in God, to the contrary, will embrace and understand the finite universe as created by the one, omnipotent, omniscient, and infinitely good God and thus as a well-ordered domain, in which the good ultimately trumps the bad, even if it is still being defaced by many sorts of evil and misery. They recognize that the world is a mixture of good and evil and that suffering belongs to human life; but they experience the good facts and aspects as normal and natural, whereas they consider the bad aspects and events to be weeds among the wheat or as corrupted by hostile powers. Apparently, the Creator has not prevented or undone the many monstrous forms of corruption that ravage this wonderful creation, but its origin and final orientation are good. Since nothing exists beyond the finite universe except God, the corrupting powers must be found within the universe (which, as totality, is finite), to begin with human freedom and the whims or vagaries of nature. But why does God not discipline those hostile powers according to the reasonable wishes and norms of our, human, rationality? Even if the culprits of evil and suffering hide in nature and our own free but ambiguous liberty—perhaps also in some demonic forms of intervention—we cannot avoid asking how the infinite Creator can want or "permit" that we must live in a hostile and failing world? How are the finite and earthly sources of corruption able to exist without being supervised and directed by the divine responsibility to which they, just as all other creatures, should entirely be subordinate? Can human or superhuman freedom resist God's intentions without being rectified, even before that freedom has a chance to revolt against the Creator's plan? Does God's will take the risk of resulting in a humanly or demonically disabled or failing work? Does the Infinite accept such a mixed result as outcome of the sovereign plan?

Whereas faith in God must find a response (but not necessarily a philosophical one) to the aporetic questions that rise from the tension between a good creation, the interference of evil, accompanied by horrendous suffering, and the infinite beauty of divine perfection, nonbelievers are challenged to explain not only the possibility of evil but also, and more basically, the universe's existence as such (and their own existence in it) without recurring to the philosophical hypothesis that nothing finite can exist unless it owes its existence to the operative existence of the one and only infinite God, as the long—not only Western—tradition of philosophy has strongly affirmed or suggested. If they recognize the challenge, no science can help them, because all sciences focus on finite entities, events, relations, or aspects of the universe, which cannot be made responsible for its own existence, or for the emergence from nothing of its components.

Only a few philosophers have tried to demonstrate the nonexistence or the impossibility of God. Many of them, however, ignore or avoid the question, while appealing to a widespread ethos of unreflected denial. But others have attacked the conviction of those who present their trust in God's existence as a necessary conclusion or postulate of their philosophical arguments. Several ways have been tried out on both sides to successfully conduct a demonstration or refutation for the adopted standpoint. Since the modern Enlightenment, a favorite attack has consisted in the attempt of showing that faith in God weakens, distorts, impedes, alienates, or destroys the believers' freedom and confidence in humanity's own capacity of fully cultivating and enjoying the world's splendid opportunities. The motivation for such refutations clearly squares with the "enlightened" ideal of autonomy and autarchy. They are meant to encourage trust and self-respect with regard to our own possibilities, while discrediting the kind of humility and obedience that seems to be part of faith in an absolutely sovereign but caring God.

If the contenders take their case seriously, there is more at stake than an intellectual disagreement. Two radically different attitudes, involving the entire affective, imaginative, intuitive, and poetic economy of their personalities are then mobilized for a genuine struggle—inside as well as outside their soul and conscience. The outcome of this struggle should be decisive for the discovery of the primordial and ultimate *meaning* of the universe and human existence in it. Trust in God, as rooted in a gratefully received and lovingly embraced dependence on infinite benevolence, is faced by the idea of a fully emancipated, self-confident humanity that believes in its mission of possessing the universe as its own obedient property.

Another, but kindred, manner of disqualifying the believers' trust in their infinitely perfect Creator has insisted on the incompatibility of their kind of trust with the monstrous mass of suffering and crimes that tortures human society and its history. The most famous format, according to which this fight was staged, was the judicial stage of a tribunal in which the prosecutors, who denied God's existence, faced defendants who tried to show that God's infinite power and wisdom cannot be guilty of the failures and crimes that deface the world. The standard title of this type of discussion expresses its character rather well by calling the defense a *Theodicea:* an attempted, yet contested, *justification* of God's creative activity.

The style of the pleas that both parties produced, was preponderantly the clear, rational, conceptual and analytic style of philosophy in its early modern version. Many concepts, definitions, axioms, and not only logical but also ontological connections were presupposed, especially with regard to the concepts of good and evil, moral goodness and enjoyment or pleasure, freedom and determinism, justice and injustice in relation to the distribution of rights, rewards, and punishments. When we look back, we might be amazed by several features of such a modern theodicy. Not only is the ease with which the participants handle the most difficult concepts surprising, it is also truly astounding that little is said about the problematic character of applying their assumptions to the infinity of God's thought and activity regarding the finitude of human individuals and humanity as a whole. Shouldn't one begin with a justification of any attempt to dissect and assemble God's actions by means of definitions and distinctions that are won in a time-consuming and empirically based study of human persons or simply borrowed from common sense? Are we, by virtue of our finite intellect, capable of analyzing the internal and external relations of the Infinite with intellect and will, love and justice, pardon and grace, or divine freedom and the human will? More than two thousand years of awareness about the *aporetic* necessity of inventing a particular brand of metaphorical and largely negative language that would permit us to transcend—at least in thoughts—the finite cosmos, seem forgotten. Or is such a naiveté an appropriate punishment for "enlightened" contempt with regard to metaphysical and metaphorical explorations?

The summit of oddity in theodicy is reached, when the participants, while forwarding their reasons and conclusions, act as if they are the judges who have to produce a verdict about God's capabilities and motivations (if God indeed exists as truly being God and not as a human fiction or supreme ghost only), or else about the nonexistence of the Good whom billions of people for many centuries have been adoring. Have those judges realized that one cannot treat God as an ignorant, incompetent, or culpable entity, whose approval or rejection should depend on human measurements? Even if one does not believe in God's existence, one cannot talk about God without at least hypothetically respecting what the word *God,* according to its most lucid worshippers, indicates. All gods and other idols can be studied and named as being encompassed by a finite horizon of logic, language, imagination, myth, and history, although even this can be too difficult or too unpleasant for many thinkers. But God does not fit within such a horizon, because only God transcends the entire universe. God is not the highest or greatest being—which would make God a part of the universe—but instead not finite at all, no part of anything else, strictly absolute. But then also adorable—not an appropriate object that can be viewed, studied, compared, analyzed, discussed, objectively determined, or defined. To speak *about* God is already to miss the only One, who is adorable, because the speakers then necessarily place themselves on a supreme standpoint, from which they look at God as if God were part of an imaginary "all-ness" (*to pan*) that must be shared with the rest of a universe that gathers all finite realities (*ta panta*). If speaking about God from such a viewpoint is the only possible way of developing a philosophical theology, then God cannot be found in philosophy; for such an objectifying perspective chases the Infinite away from the all-encompassing map.

However, another stance and attitude is more appropriate to encountering the God who transcends the all of the universe. And here we must oppose a second oddity of several theodicies: their authors are so concentrated on the conceptual puzzles to which they reduce the scandal of omnipresent corruption and horrendous suffering that they hardly seem to suffer from that scandal. If their discussions were serious, would their struggle with one another and their own doubts then not be experienced as a tremendous drama? Are they not excited—profoundly afraid or joyfully energized—by the thought that this drama will develop into the worst of all tragedies or else—in the name of hope—into the most trustworthy assurance that we are already embraced by the infinitely good, wise, just, capable, and saving power of the only One who can save us from evil and nonsense?

Philosophers who believe that God exists have given us rational arguments that can be checked and approved or faulted and rejected, but their audience can remain very cold and emotionally untouched, perhaps even rather indifferent. Is this not an inevitable result of the purely conceptual procedures that have transformed the indicated scandal into an exclusively theoretical problem? How can this problem be reconducted to its existential proportions?

As soon as we are really hit by the contradiction between a glorious earth and its corruption through many kinds of evil, followed by atrocious forms of suffering, we are in an affective turmoil. Despite all that can be said about the reasonableness or the necessity of trust in fellow people, nature, society, or human history, we do and must ask: Does our world, does existence—our existence and all that is involved in it—still warrant or, at least, deserve trust? Is—in the end, ultimately, fundamentally, radically—trust the only correct response to the mixture with which we are confronted, or should suspicion and distrust be a more adequate response to our factual situation here and now and eventually, probably, in the future?

The existential struggle for an appropriate response to the present predicament has deeper—experiential, intuitive, affective, and motivational—roots than a merely conceptual one that proceeds by reason alone. Those philosophers who bracket or ignore those roots must already have found a position for or against God and radical trust, or they are waiting, still undecided, somewhere in between. Have they been disturbed and shocked? Some of them might feel so well at home in their faith (which goes much deeper and encompasses much more than a combination of beliefs) that they see their logical explications as a clarifying transposition of their deepest conviction onto the level of philosophical rationality, without forgetting their existential involvement in the shocking and tragic aspects of the real problems. Whatever someone's position may be, trust in the course of the universe and trust or distrust in God are more radical manners of being at home in the world than logically exact conclusions of well-reasoned arguments. If trust in God is serious and if trust in a universe that does not refer to any beyond is equally radical, these different trusts will permeate the entire personality of the involved, including their emotional economy and the entire climate that characterizes their emotional, practical, and epistemic activity.

If those who do not believe in a divine creator put their trust in any finite reality—matter, life, power, money, pleasure, demons, gods, science, art, some hidden, mysterious force, or the universe as a whole—their orientation will be seen as idolatrous by those who oppose them in the name of their faith in one uniquely infinite God. Can the latter be certain about their faith? If they do take God seriously, they express this by adopting adoration as their basic stance,[9] while relativizing all attempts at defining and demonstrating God's essence and existence. Instead of capturing God as center or summit of a conceptual network, they thank the Origin of heaven-and-earth for their own existence together with all the other gifts implied in their dwelling on earth and under the heaven. Because they feel profoundly grateful for the radical and overwhelming gift of emerging from nothing into their own, singular and completely undeserved existence, including all the abundance and trustworthy regularity of an awe-inspiring world, they also accept the abnormal and shocking exceptions, disasters, disappointments, and tragic events that happen to them and their fellow humans. Conscious of the incomparable distance between their own—wholly dependent, received, and limited—mode of being, doing, acting, and knowing, they try to understand why evil and suffering belong to their mortal existence, yet even the most shocking and tragic events do not ruin their most radical trust. Conscious of their own failures and sins, they do not become suspicious of a divine version of incompetence and certainly do not crush their awe and adoration by summoning God to appear in a judicial drama. Well aware of their own, not quite innocent responses to the gift of being created for an enjoyable existence, they would accept the greatest tragedies and disasters, even without understanding them, rather than railing against the Origin or returning their entrance ticket to existence. (To whom or to what would they send it?) To withdraw into death would only augment the horror of their despair.

In order to cope with suffering and sin, the faithful find more trustworthy meaning and consolation in religion than in philosophy, especially if the religious message is forwarded in an authentic way. Certain philosophers, especially some great classics, may also be convincing, but those who narrow their philosophy to the bare, cold bones of conceptual reasoning alone, will not generate enough sympathy to be listened to without end.

Plato's recourse to myths is a good example of a philosopher who broadened his scope by finding inspiration in religious texts for the most difficult questions of his philosophy. In line with Paul Ricoeur's *Symbolique du Mal,*[10] we might borrow some hints from biblical myths; for example from those with which the Bible begins and to which we already have turned earlier while meditating on the possibility of radical trust.

The first of these myths unrolls a poetic description of God's spoken Word that, in a well-planned sequence, evokes all elementary, vegetal, animal, and human existence out of nothing in order to replace an undetermined emptiness with a glorious cosmos that harbors a human paradise. The relations that thus emerge between God and humanity are ideal and they would have remained such, if nothing disastrous had happened on the human side.[11] The second myth,[12] however, tells how the projected agreement was never realized because it was aborted by the first and fatal tragedy of all tragedies. Before we could fully enjoy our fortunate and immortal destiny in friendship with the Creator, the cosmos, and humanity as a whole, we failed to embrace it.

The myth invites us to see ourselves ("Adam") as created and placed under the protection of two trees: the tree of life, which guarantees immortality, and the tree of supreme discernment regarding the abyssal difference between the truly good and the truly bad. The latter tree symbolizes the supreme, definitive wisdom that decides about the meaning of all that exists and promulgates the Law according to which we ought to develop. This supreme wisdom is rooted in the absolute sovereignty of God. We are forbidden to eat from it, because our responsibility is a union of freedom and listening, not the absolute form of originary and absolute sovereignty. However, we are tempted and seduced by a mysterious animal: the "serpent," who suggests that God has lied in telling us about the link between the one most radical prohibition and human mortality. Our attempt at replacing God's sovereign wisdom with our own originates all sin and suffering. That is the answer to our illusion of redoing the creation by planning a humanly produced, more understandable, controllable, and comfortable world than the one that was offered as the original, natural, normal, and perfectly good one.

Our attempt at stealing God's sovereignty has changed the exhilarating adventure of our undivided friendship with God and one another into an ongoing tragedy. Excluded from the tree of life, we live in a compromised and corrupted world, disfigured by idolatry, hostility, suffering, and death. The revolt against God's originary supremacy has disturbed not only our religious familiarity with God and the universe, but also our social and political relations, as the immediate following myth about Cain's murder of his innocent brother Abel illustrates.[13]

Human self-divinization, root of all idolizations, generates interhuman envy, hatred, violence, discrimination, wars, terror, genocide, and all the global—colonial, capitalist, communist, and other—systems of robbery and slavery. The Bible abounds in stories that intimately connect trust in idols (which implies detachment from the only One who creates) with moral, political, and religious disasters, thus confirming in many ways that replacement of trust in the Creator (which implies a recognition of humanity's utter dependence) with a human caricature of divine sovereignty generates universal misery. Fortunately, this consequence is not the end of divine creation, which still persists thanks to the trustworthy loyalty and grace of the true Sovereign, but the compromised remains of paradise are marked by the persistence of corrupting factors and events.

The myth of the fall suggests that the wounded world in which we live—a splendid one, but tainted by corruption—owes its wounds to our sins, but we might find a partial excuse in the fact that we are seduced by the serpent's false yet specious refutation of God's command.[14] Obviously such an excuse does not disculpate the perpetrator of the crime, but the mention of a tempting force seems phenomenologically correct: we are not the absolute inventors of evil, but rather its heirs, seduced by powerful traditions that are quite difficult to rectify. The ethos that dominates our historically grown context, for example, contains a dangerous mixture of good and bad incentives. At the same time we have a vaguely melancholic feeling that we ourselves—perhaps more collectively than individually—are somehow responsible for the corruption that has spoiled an originarily intended, but never quite realized, paradise.

The imaginative stories of *Genesis* 1–4 seem to mirror fairly well a basic tenet of classic philosophy, which states that all forms of evil (with their terrifying consequences) are secondary with regard to a preceding, originary, pure, and genuine, not yet faked, distorted, falsified, or betrayed, good. Good and evil are not two kinds of one universal category. The good is proper to being in its original and purest form, whereas evil is defined since Plato as a "lack": a *privation boni,* as the medieval philosophers called it. This lack is not just an absence, but instead a missed presence or the incorrect and condemnable absence (or nonbeing or destruction) of a good that *ought to be* present. Evil is the perversion of a good that—alas!—is corrupted, poisoned, distorted, destroyed, or prevented, although it essentially belongs to and should accompany or express the genuine good it betrays. If this "definition" is correct, evil is not a total annihilation of the good that is harmed or curtailed by it, but instead a stain or wound, a corrupting or destructive aspect or caricature of a reality that, as (created) being, still keeps at least some of its "natural" and normal goodness and existence.

With regard to the question of suffering, we must recognize that we do not have a clear insight in the reasons why and by whom or what so much of it is caused in our history, although we can understand that at least part of it is due to a wrong orientation and "use" of human freedom. We are vaguely aware that our own transgressions have something to do with the tragic aspect of our world's darkened and ambiguous existence, but suffering and cruelty remain surrounded by a painful mystery. As far as trust is concerned, however, it is important to note that a glorious universe remains possible, insofar as the good and enjoyable side of our existence is not annulled but only obfuscated, distorted, wounded, and partially corrupted, while we keep groping toward a renewal that might be given through pardon and regeneration.

To our perplexities, we must add that suffering, however distressing it may be, is not always wholly bad or meaningless. Like all human actions, a victim's undergoing of suffering, inflicted, for example, by a torturer, *can* at the same time be a supreme, most admirable (though still regrettable) expression of loyalty, service, love, or dedication. The "passion" of martyrs and other heroes of justice, liberation, prophesy or sanctity expresses the victims' loving attachment to their noble cause. The trust that motivates their courage transforms the violence done to them into the strongest possible testimony for their cause. Their example might encourage us to stick to the trust that has become ours after due consideration of available responses to the world's and our own tragedies or regrets.

DOES OUR UNIVERSE DESERVE TRUST?

Getting to know the world and ourselves ends the naivety of early confidence. Evil and suffering not only surround us but also corrupt us from within. They have a real presence inside and out and without end. Here lies perhaps one of the main differences between our evaluation and the evaluation documented by much of the eighteenth- and nineteenth-century literature. With the political and economical disasters that have occurred since the nineteenth century and the cultural crisis that then gradually became visible, suspicion and distrust have made great advances. Even the media focus today more on disasters and scandals than on successes, luck, and progress. Although we sometimes hear and read about persons and associations that are admirably dedicated to alleviating the sufferings of the poor and victimized, the myth of ongoing progress in human generosity has been muted and the general mood is more attuned to fear and trembling than to gratitude and hope. Overdoses of silly entertainment are, of course, bad surrogates for tasteful confidence, but also expressions of decadence and empty despair.

When naïveté makes place for a more enlightened awareness of the extent to which evil and suffering permeate our world, the question of trust versus distrust becomes a huge problem. We cannot give up the basic trust that was always there; but should we not feel anguished because of our being caught in well-established systems of arrogance, greed, contempt, and hatred? And to what extent can we still trust ourselves, if we are so easily seduced to collaboration with such systems?

How should we feel as more or less informed inhabitants of this world at this moment of its history? The omnipresence of suffering, death, guilt, and destruction from AIDS and murders through all sorts of addictions to endless wars and ecological crimes; the dominion of capitalist exploitation, slavery, and colonization; the cruelty of dictators; the guilt of our personal misdeeds; and our vague yet real participation in the common culpability—all these and similar phenomena together form a disorderly mixture. The question of whether we should trust or distrust this ensemble seems unanswerable because of its extreme confusion.

Do anguish or even global condemnation and general disgust dictate our reaction? If that were the case, we would be blind for all the good and beautiful—and sometimes glorious—aspects of human existence that likewise must be recognized. Although the world is being crucified, the pain of it does not abolish the admiration it still deserves. Moreover, signs of revival, rebirth, renaissance, and resurrection appear time and again. Pain and mourning cannot annul our celebration of the earth. They would even lose their meaning if they did not testify to the also existing glories of present and past and the hopefully expected reality of new jubilations. Between anguish and hope or between mourning and renaissance, we want trust to win, although we are realistic enough to recognize that paradise is only a dream. However, if evil is a perversion, its total victory would not make sense, because we cannot stop trusting that the good is ultimately stronger, as it was also more original.

If distrust were the only possible or the best answer to our being born into the world in which we must live until death, which motivation would justify this attitude? What threatens us in our very existence? If death were nothing else than a return to dust or nonexistence, such a transition would be disappointing insofar as our being holds fast onto itself and wants to prolong its existence against destruction. Death would then mean nothing more than a loss, but does this justify the deepest of all anxieties? Is a finite period of human life no opportunity at all, because it is not eternal? It would be regrettable if the opportunity *in the end* were without meaning, empty, or completely superfluous. It would be even worse, however, if the opportunity was used for causing pain or guilt to others or oneself, and worst of all if a bad life were followed by punishment or eternal suffering.

Evil is certainly worse and more threatening than mortality and the pain of suffering, because it is a distortion and (at least a partial) destruction of meaning, and not only of being there or of the joy that normally adheres to this. Among all evils, guilt is the summit of being unfortunate, because one can neither undo its cause nor erase the guilt itself without being forgiven by someone who makes a new beginning possible (But is such a new beginning possible without a recreation?).

Religion promises answers to the questions that emerge from meditation about the trustworthiness of human existence on the earth. Can mortality be absorbed by eternity? Can we escape a final destruction, terminal meaninglessness, an endlessly ongoing mixture of enjoyable good and dreadful evil? Is a purification possible that leads to a new kind of innocence? Even without paying attention to religions, we currently speak of forgiving, pardon, recovered innocence, renaissance, second naïveté and everlasting significance, but are such phrases more than secularized reminiscences of presecularized times? Do they only name nice but cheating dreams?

Tempted by generalized anxiety but still hoping that human existence, after all and for the most part, is worthy of a cautious kind of trust, we seek an adequate balance of trust and distrust with regard to the world and ourselves. But which lonely and multiply threatened individual can solve such a gigantic problem?

RELIGION-BASED TRUST

Many myths and grand narratives, powerful traditions, books of wisdom, and prophetic kerygmas have emerged to guide individuals, families and communities in their search for an adequate response to the mixture of good and evil in which they are steeped. Because the question regards the foundations of human existence, it is a religious question in the broad sense of "religion," as dimension of the basic and most serious human engagement. Besides the great religions, which figure in all encyclopedias of religion, that broad sense of *religion* encompasses also all other modes of communal affection, praxis, and knowledge that present themselves as answers to the truly fundamental and ultimate interests of human existence. *Philosophia,* in the original sense of a search for existential wisdom, has then also a religious character and, as such, it sometimes offers itself as an alternative to the basic convictions of Jewish, Christian, Muslim, Hindu, Buddhist, or other explicitly religious faiths.

Should religion guide individuals who ask in whom and what they should invest their basic trust and distrust? Must we, to answer this question, not discover first which one of the many religions we can or cannot trust? In chapter 6, we saw that modern philosophy pretends to be capable of proving which truths should determine our fundamental orientation, but I also claimed that such proofs have never been delivered. All philosophers do rely on some hypotheses, sometimes called axioms, not only by way of a strategic or didactic maneuver, which they later will justify by demonstrating the truth of those axioms, but because they deem them trustworthy, even if they are not able to prove them.

The same is true of all religions, of course, and few or none of them pretend that their stories, myths, or prophecies are provable theses of some science or learned theory. They offer their credibility as shown and tested by the lived reality of their own practice and self-understanding. Christianity, for example, does not present itself as a theoretical system, based on scientifically established and analyzed data, which then are connected through logically warranted arguments, but rather as a creditworthy, reasonable, convincing, well-fitting, inspiring, and moving message and historical practice that speaks for itself, while assuring the listeners that God's love invites them to an adequate response. The mixture of praxis and conviction to which they are invited does not have the character of a demonstration; instead, it testifies to a specific form of trust (*pistis*), faith (*fides*), and fidelity. If attentive listeners are moved by that message, because they deem it credible and lovable, they feel otherwise and more profoundly fortunate than a philosopher or scientist who has proved the most important and difficult theorem of his or her career. In faith they have encountered the most important love of their life—which at the same time is the greatest love one can have for humanity and all individuals of which it is composed.[15]

DOES RELIGIOUS FAITH JUSTIFY TRUST?

The perspective that has framed my description of the human milieu was determined by the contrast between trust and distrust, which is central in this book: To what extent can we trust the factual universe of our existence and entrust our lives to it? This question takes on an urgent tone, when we realize how much our universe, and consequently our own existence, as completely unpredictable gifts, are overwhelmed by an abundance of good and beautiful, heart- and intellect-warming treasures, but also infiltrated by pain, suffering, hostility, destruction, hatred, abuse, and hypocrisy. If we insist on the latter aspect,[16] mustn't we then conclude that distrust or even despair form a more adequate response than a basic and global trust, without which we cannot live? It is tempting to seek a way out of this aporia in the direction of a saving power, which hates and destroys evil in order to replace it with enjoyable realizations of the Good. However, various difficulties besiege such a solution.

First of all, evil facts or events of the past or present cannot be undone; they remain true for all eternity. Perhaps their motivations can be forgiven, but their unjust and destructive efficacy cannot be nullified. In an interview, Martin Heidegger declared that "only a god can save us," but who feels saved when remembering the myriads of old—Sumerian, Babylonian, Assyrian, Egyptian, Greek, Roman, Germanic—gods (many of whom were not that benevolent, while all of them are very dead) or their fake imitations of more recent times?

However, some interlocutor might answer: "Why should your Christian God be a more trustworthy savior than Osiris, Isis, Kronos, Zeus, Dionysius, Apollo, or Prometheus?"

At this point, we could begin to discuss the abyssal differences between faith in one unique, absolute, and infinite God and all forms of polytheism. If God is the unique creator and ultimate savior, the word *God* loses that meaning altogether in order to become a homonym, when it is applied to a multiplicity of gods. Whereas such a multiplicity loudly proclaims the finitude of the gods, the one and only God does not permit confinement to any genus, class, or universe, of which God would be a member. No Jew, Christian, or Muslim puts his or her deepest trust in any god or other imitation of the unique and only One, who transcends all images and concepts of the divine. To compare God with Zeus or Dionysos is possible only within a framework of idolatry.

My interlocutor might interrupt me here by asking the question of how an orthodox faith in God differs from trust in Homeric gods or those of the Roman pantheon. Is trust in the universe better founded in monotheism than in a Homeric or Egyptian world? Does your God deliver better protection against death, suffering, and other forms of evil, more brilliant or amazing miracles, a more peaceful future, and so on, than Athena, Poseidon, Zeus, and all the others? The answer is summarized in sacred traditions about Abel, Moses, Elijah, Jeremiah, Job, Jesus, and so many other humiliated and slaughtered saints.

But, if faith does not guarantee protection against injustice and suffering, why then should one prefer to believe and trust in the one God of Jews, Christians, or Muslims? If the motivation of our faith consists in the hope that God will prevent humanity from all harm or hatred, we are apparently mistaken.

Obviously the question of trusting God cannot be restricted to our wish or need to be freed from all evils, some of which were mentioned above. God is not only a savior—even if indeed a unique one, who has a unique, and often mysterious, way of saving—but first of all the creator and providence of "heaven and earth." As infinite, and thus neither a god nor the universe, God apparently does not eliminate our mortality or criminality, but mysteriously "keeps" the universe of human history "in his hands" and "under his wings"—as a psalm-singing Jew or Christian would express it.

Does the world of religious faith then differ from the world of an agnostic or God-denying person?[17]

Yes and no. *No,* because faith does not add supplemental features to the world of scientific observation and experimentation, and because faith is not a more excellent or competing form of scientific or philosophical theory. Faith is not primarily a source of knowledge, belief, or opinion, although the truths it implies illuminate the world and our existence in it.

And therefore: *Yes,* faith is a trusting attachment to the perfect truth, and this changes everything. In faith, as confidential adherence to God, the world "comes to light" in a horizon or "light" that is entirely *different but not separate* from all perceptive, scientific, aesthetic, hedonic, poetic, or utilitarian lights that appear when the world is (falsely?) experienced as given by nothing else than itself. By abolishing not only all gods and pseudo-Gods, but also God, an atheist is forced to perceive and think the universe as a self-giving, self-supporting, and self-enlightening *causa sui.* Whereas religious faith delivers the universe from all tendencies to self-divinization, a world that claims to be its own origin tries to hide its givenness and forbids all search beyond its own abundance and deficiency. It consequently elicits another form of amazement from its admirers than the universe of those who receive it as the greatest gift from the incomparable Giver who is traced and signified in it. Believers see—or rather read and hear—the world as the word that God speaks to them, or—as the medieval thinkers said—as a book in which they try to decode the symbolic presence of the Writer, who addresses them in it.[18] The position of our universe as mediation in our relation to its unique and incomparable but adorable Origin makes all the difference between religious faith and all other perspectives—scientific, poetic, or other. The latter remain confined to the horizon of universality, without reaching beyond the universe in order to get at least a glimpse of the Origin, who, as *absolutely different but not separate,* dwells in it.

Indeed, universality, the principle of all theory, does liberate our mind from all obsessions and fixations on individual and particular subjects. It opens us for "all that is" (*ta panta*) and "the all" (*to pan*), as Parmenides, the father of all philosophers, already understood, but Plato discovered that universality is neither the end nor the beginning of thought, because the totality of all ideas and entities must be conditioned by one source—and not a multiplicity of sources—which he called "the Good." This helped Jewish, Christian, and Muslim philosophers to translate their biblical faith in the one and unique Creator of heaven and earth into a philosophical language. A profound difference between biblical faith and Greek theory remains, however. Plato contemplates, while admiring the composition of the universe in its dependence on its ultimate Principle, whereas Jews, Christians, and Muslims pray before and after—and in some sense even during—all other activities, including the theoretical ones. For them, an adequate relation to the Origin is always essential, even in performing their loftiest flights of exploration of the universe and their own involvement in it. The truth of the universe thus can be separated neither from its being given, spoken, written and addressed to us, nor from our response to this amazing gift, which is perhaps more similar to a letter than to a finished book.

FAITH IN GOD AS TRUST

How some atheists, after millennia of religious education, can avoid scrutinizing the world as an amazing ensemble of invitations to search for the mystery of the giving that hides in them, is not easy to understand. For how could the cosmic multiplicity, if it were the horizon of all horizons and the light of all lights, claim to be also the ground of all grounds or the cause of all causes, including itself? The only possibility of maintaining one's balance in front of such a miracle seems to lie in a choice between two positions: either to declare the cosmos itself primordial and ultimate or divine (which may reintroduce a pantheon of fragmentary gods), or to declare that the first and all-encompassing question of thinking—what is the *archē,* the *ground,* the *principle,* the *cause?*—is misleading, impossible, mistaken, or forbidden.[19]

Although faith in God is not conditioned by any scientific or philosophical knowledge, most believers are in excellent company when they—like Plato, Aristotle, Plotinus, Descartes, Spinoza, Leibniz, Malebranche, Kant, and Hegel—assume that, even outside their religious communities, most people take the necessary existence of a pre- or super-human and pre- or super-cosmic principle (or "God") for granted. Whether they formulate this assumption in mythical, ritual, poetic, quasi-scientific, philosophical, or outright theological language—and which of such languages are the most adequate—is not the main point here. It is not even necessary to have any language for the final and primordial mystery, because even the mute and deaf point to the ultimate through the silent longing of their most intimate *desire.* For, indeed, which meaning or which *desideratum* can satisfy a human soul, if the horizon—or the original "light" that shines in it—is unlimited and nonfinite in the strongest sense of the word *infinity*?

However, it is rarely a philosophical process in the puzzled mind that has brought the faithful to their deepest convictions. Most often it is their belonging to a certain community—a family, a church, a circle of friends or colleagues, a religious or charitable movement—whose mode of attunement, concern, belonging, worshipping, serving, and testifying has suggested, invited, or confirmed their attachment. Especially the intimate connection of fraternal behavior toward all fellow humans with loyalty to the God whose love guarantees the lovability of all is often experienced as the secret—or mystery—of religion.

If faith is not some particular knowledge, but instead the most fundamental attachment to God *and* all members of humanity, *all religions* are attempts at expressing this core attachment that gives rise to the symbolic, affective, imaginative, reflexive, and linguistic diversity of human cultures.

If the above is true, the Christian's stance,[20] expressed in a particular mode of dealing with others and the world, differs profoundly from all positions whose ultimate horizon is limited to a merely spatiotemporal, imaginative, or speculative horizon of the universe. In faith, the ultimate horizon is God alone as creator, savior, and definitive future of the human universe.

Whereas the universe (including its gods and demons) is not only a totality, and consequently a *finite* whole, but also tainted by *perversions,* God's revelation orients humanity toward the One who, surpassing all finitude and evil, gives access to the freedom of an infinite goodness that does not despise the existence of mortal, plagued and failing men and women. Indeed, God's incarnation includes the tragedy of resistance, hatred and murder, as the lives of Jesus and many saints before and after him have shown. But Christians testify to life's divine infinity by celebrating the glory of Christ's resurrection as summary of the human destination.

As members of a community that understands itself as living "in Christ," because it is animated by his and "the Father's" Spirit, Christians feel established in the trust of all trusts, if they remain loyal to their rebirth into that community of resurrection. The language in which they express their confidence in God, is metaphoric and full of negations because the divine reality in which they participate escapes all languages, for these are better adjusted to the universe of finite categories and correlations than to an evocation of God's infinity.

Faith is not comparable to any science or philosophy; it is not even equivalent to any dogma or theology, because these are already imaginative, rhetorical, logical, or ontological *translations* of a lived reality that transcends all culture. Faith in God is not a version of "theism," not only because it escapes all *isms,* but, more profoundly, because it precedes and surpasses all theological and other formulations. Underneath our words and declarations, faith is the silent, but potentially eloquent, returning home of an unconscious familiarity with the invisible presence of God in all things.

When Christians confess that they believe *in* God, this does not mean that they consider certain propositions or articles of faith correct or true, but rather that they confide their entire lives to the caring God, whose calling in the form of revealing signs they answer by turning to Him in grateful recognition of his creative abundance and saving compassion. That God neither takes any grandeur from humans away, nor alienates or enslaves anyone, but instead gives life, love, creativity, and resurrection to them is a glorious truth, but it does not represent a philosophical theorem, which skillfully should or could be dissected, tested, confirmed, doubted, proved, or refuted. All articles of faith are integral elements of a relation that commits the affections and the will—or the heart—of the faithful. For faith, like all trust, implies more than a list or system of affirmative statements; it attaches a person to the God who always already has loved all that exists from before the possibility of its existence. The faithful know that they always come late in discovering and accepting their existence as a gift for which they cannot thank adequately enough, because it overwhelms their desire of being safe and fortunate within the horizon of a universe that, despite its tragic failures and its ridiculous conceits, owes its being to the only one unfathomably lovable and loving God.[21]

To believe *in* God, and not only *that* many truths regarding God are true, belongs to the class of expressions that not only involve a movement *toward* someone but also entrust the trusted person with (at least a part or aspect or function of) the truster's own life. To trust you is to make you participate in the development of my own existence, as explained in chapter 2. If I put my most basic and all-encompassing trust in God, I entrust myself to the One who entrusts me with my-self, while confirming and enriching the meaning of this self as a generously given, gratefully received, and hopefully confided gift. Because the gift itself coincides with the whole of me—including those components of the world that condition the course of my existence—faith, as trust in God, is the total return of a radical confidence that does not leave anything out: "Into your hands I commit the entirety of my life."[22]

Because the course of each singular life is conditioned by a host of relations with other lives and the shared world thanks to which we exist, faith in the one God of all beings colors and deepens all natural and social realities, with which we are dealing. The immensity of the cosmos, including the human society and its entire history, appears in faith as a symbolic universe of signs, expressions, poems, novels, and dramas, in which—as through hazy mirrors and enigmatic codes—God's *will* or *design* is waiting for faith-guided deciphering. Great liturgies and works of art have testified to the trustworthiness of that hidden meaning. Saint Francis's canticle on Brother Sun and Dante's *Divina Comedia* are two summits of such confident adoration, but myriads of other narrative, poetic, architectonic, musical, and sacramental celebrations of the same faith will encourage us, if we pay attention.

It is not possible to develop here a theological compendium of Christian faith, but hopefully enough has been said to introduce the following summary. If God exists as creator and savior, one may trust in the course and meaning of our earthly past and future, including our ways of dealing with human death and all other disasters of nature and history. As participants in God's creative and saving and always reinspiring work, we are invited to cooperate in the providential, pardoning and renovating care for the course of all human lives within the world community. Insofar as we fail to do this, we need forgiveness from God and humanity because we too have participated in destructive, unloving, antihuman and antidivine moods and practices.

Only a radical liberation can undo our undoing, if freedom implies pardon. Since God is revealed as forgiving, trust in renewed innocence is possible. Insofar as we cannot prevent certain evils that happen to others and ourselves, however, we cannot escape suffering. But the worst forms of suffering lack all justification and explanation. Since faith includes loyalty, even without explanation ("your judgment is not ours"), such suffering, too, must be accepted. Inexplicable suffering is *the hardest* test of our fidelity, but even that can be endured, if a strong enough trust is granted. Such a trust seems blind. Or is it ignited and infused by a blinding light?

ATHEIST TRUST AND DISTRUST: DID GOD BECOME AN IDOL?

During millennia, faith in God has been proclaimed and heeded as the secret of a good, blessed, and blessing-worthy life. Some time ago, however, certain intellectuals began to deny the validity of that faith by denying the existence of God. After some eighteenth-century atheists, Feuerbach, Marx, Nietzsche, and Sartre are perhaps the most often mentioned authors in this context. The God they rejected was a God, who, according to *their* understanding, had dominated the European culture with which they deemed themselves acquainted, but the reasons for their rejection were not exclusively theoretical; allegations of harms caused by human belief in God played a major role.

Neither a genealogy nor a diagnosis of atheism can be given in this book, but at least a few remarks may be expected about the question of which sort of trust may satisfy the generally recognized axiom according to which we cannot live without any basic trust with regard to the main conditions of a meaningful existence. For philosophers and theologians, it is obvious that some of the "Gods" rejected by various kinds of atheists are rather different from the God(s) of Plato, Plotinus, Augustine, Aquinas, Eckhart, Cusanus, Descartes, Leibniz, Malebranche, Kant, Blondel, Bergson, Marcel, Levinas, and almost all philosophical classics until Hegel, but similar differences might also divide less learned believers. Regrettably some mediocre interpreters of the Christian faith can be quoted to justify attacks on a God, who steals freedom, power, insight, mental health, and joy from human beings, whose trust in God, according to their accusers, would alienate them from themselves and humanity. A serious engagement with philosophy or theology, however, shows how difficult it already is to "simply" agree on the meaning of the name *God*, not to mention the predicates one can use to evoke God's relation to humanity and the world.

The pathos with which some atheists have attacked faith in the God(s) of Greek philosophers and Christian, Jewish, or Muslim faithful demands an explanation. If they use philosophical arguments in order to prove that God does *not* or even cannot exist, they can be refuted philosophically, and with ease. If their attacks on certain preachers are philosophically justified, one has to point out that these messengers either distort the authentic message or that they are misinterpreted by their attackers. If the latter ask a positive proof of God's existence from those who put their trust in this existence, an answer emerges by stating that our most radical trust does not depend on any philosophical demonstration (if that were a condition, more than 99 percent of humanity would be excluded from faith), and that it is controversial among philosophers whether a rigorous proof of God's existence is possible at all.

If God is infinite, and therefore absolutely different from the universe (which may be endlessly varied in quantity and quality—and consequently utterly finite, despite its immeasurable extensions), then God cannot be discovered, described, analyzed, or derived in the same way or according to the same methods as finite entities, parts, or wholes. God can neither be discovered as existing behind, among, underneath, beside, or on top of other beings within the horizon of one total universe, nor deduced through conceptual analyses, derivations, conceptual linkages, or syllogistic arguments. In other words, the Infinite cannot emerge from any argument that determines and distinguishes different entities (which, as distinct, are necessarily limited and finite) in order to relate them by distinct (and thus finite) links. What can be deduced is either a part of the universe or the universe itself as the totality of all parts. As a composite reality, the totality of all parts coincides with the togetherness of the finite components and their mutual links. Consequently the universe is as finite as its components. To call the whole or the synthesis composed by these components *God,* because of its immensity in some spatiotemporal, mathematical, conceptual, or ontological sense, would be to erect an enormous, all-encompassing system, idol, or highest god. This would then surpass all other wholes and syntheses in quantity, quality, energy, and influence, but it still lacks God's incomparable absoluteness and infinity. And the gap between God and the universe cannot be closed by any method or logic that fits the reality of finite things or thoughts. Another kind of transcendence is needed here.[23]

If the existence of God cannot be derived from any combination of finite beings or ideas, it is *a fortiori* evident that no scientific derivation can give an answer to the question of whether God exists or not. This conclusion might be attacked by those scientific or philosophical scholars who claim that theoretical research implies an unlimited openness and most profound interest in the absolutely fundamental and ultimate question(s) of science and philosophy. It seems indeed obvious that such interest should motivate as much all scholars who are eager to discover the final answers as all other men or women who desire to know what or who might justify a most fundamental trust in the ultimate meaning of their own and others' existence. When this interest motivates the desire to prove God's existence according to the conditions of the most rigorous logic, we must realize that any consideration of God as a provable object (in the emphatic sense of *object* explained in chapter 1) inevitably misses its target. The objectifying attitude, expressed in all forms of study, demonstration, science, or logic that treat their subject matter from a freestanding, noninvolved standpoint is inadequate for an encounter with God, if it is not at the same time oriented by and embedded in a looking up that longs for God's self-presentation. Only if one is directed by an attitude that—at least hypothetically—takes into account and does justice to God's lovable and loving infinity, the sought can be met. The idea that a proof of God's objective existence should *precede* any real or tentative attachment, trust or love, is a scientific or philosophistic prejudice and one of the greatest obstacles for getting involved with God. If the attempt at finding God does not emerge from an attitude that—as seeking, looking up, and longing—is more similar to prayer than to an investigation, one might discover a principle of all principles, but still remain without any One to trust.

If some atheists consider the signaled impossibility of deducing God as a concession that confirms their own negative belief, they forget that there are other ways of reflection to confirm or disprove a trust that is born from experience, history, tradition, or contemplation, and that they themselves must explain on which ground they put their basic trust in the human universe. What is their philosophical, anti- or atheological answer to the question of ultimate trust or distrust? Or do they refuse to consider this question as unwise and irrational?

To pursue the second point first: Some atheists will counter the claim just stated by denying that it is they who should prove anything because they do not see the need of any primordial, ultimate, or absolute foundation for whatever exists. Perhaps they do not have any trust in human existence as such or they are not aware of any problem about it. If they do rely on a certain trust that human existence must have or may acquire a finite and temporal, albeit minimal meaning, they may answer the question of its basis by giving a variety of answers. They can, for instance, point at their being part of and contributing to the future of humanity, history, life itself, nature, and their own destiny. Or they might deny the possibility of acquiring valid knowledge about metaphysical or ontological problems, while accepting moral forms of meaning that they deem valid enough to justify their existence without recourse to any divine support. But whatever answer they present, it will imply that the entire context of their universe is finite *and* sufficient to fulfill their desire of meaning. They probably consider all speaking about a first principle of all principles or an absolute and infinite horizon either nonsensical or an empty dream, even if they still may use those words in some metaphorical sense to refer beyond their finite meanings. In a way, their stance is heroic, insofar as they accept their own and all other persons' and worlds' groundless and total dependence, without feeling supported by a persistent basis and without hope that the universe and life itself are meaningfully supported by some primordial and ultimate mystery.

But what is the motivation behind the aggressive atheism of the militants? For most of those who came after Hegel, belief in God implied a human loss. In their view, faith generated alienation, self-humiliation, enslavement, psychiatric problems, infantilization, and so on. They presented God and humanity as competitors: the more greatness, power, and vital and spiritual wealth is attributed to God, the more it is taken away from humanity. It might be true that some or many Christian preachers have spoken in this vein, but that was then a betrayal of the authentic tradition according to which "the glory of God coincides with the full completion of human life."

OTHER GODS?

It is understandable that, if God is eliminated, one looks into the direction of such powerful realities as Nature, Life, History, or, perhaps, some mysterious Energy or Will or Power in order to justify one's basic trust. However, it is very difficult to justify the thesis that such powers are able to replace the God of the religious traditions. More convincing motifs are necessary for founding a replacement of religion on such (new or very old) powers (or "gods"), as proclaimed by solitary messengers without support from a sacred community or a historically grown tradition. Even *Being* does not seem able to take over what God has meant for the religious history of human kind. For, if Being is understood as the being (*einai, esse*) of all beings (*onta, entia*) that populate the universe, then it must be a part or element of this same, finite universe. How then could it be its source? At least, one should get an inkling of Being's giving transcendence, as distinct from the universal givenness of "the all." Hegel identified God, as absolute Spirit, with the absolute Whole (the universe), but—as argued above—such identification makes his God as finite as the totality of its unfolding determinations.

Yet *Being* sounds interesting. Several Christian philosophers have also stated that God—and they mean the God of Christ, while using philosophical terms—is "*Being itself*" (*esse ipsum*), but they understand this expression as synonymous with the "most *actual*" and truly *infinite* "*esse*" that radically transcends the *common* being of all beings (which, as multiple, are finite). If certain atheists would trust this absolute and infinite Being itself, those Christian philosophers could welcome them as referring to the same God under another name. However, it is not likely that atheist critics would stop opposing their Being to the Christian, Jewish, or Muslim God. In any case, the faithful would still emphasize that their own philosophical names for God are only a pale reflection of the Biblical or Koranic references to the supraconceptual majesty of the living Creator whose Spirit fulfills heaven and earth.

IS THERE A PHILOSOPHICAL WAY TO GOD?

If a deduction of God's existence is not possible, are there other philosophically acceptable ways leading to God? The Platonic tradition has persisted in sketching an ascent of the human mind toward God, as the One who is the ultimate Good, but this ascent can also be read as the most profound descent toward the origin (*archē*) or source (*pēgē*) of the universe. Because the universe can neither ground itself nor contain or imply the all-surpassing and all-originating Infinite, any transition from the universe to God demands an enormous leap, which cannot be bridged by a logic of finitude. The consequence is that God's being can be affirmed—or rather, confirmed—only if the idea of God is somehow already given: either by an original—albeit deeply hidden and preconscious—acquaintance, presentiment, or desire, or else by a message that uses narrative, poetic, or sapiential metaphors to orient the human mind toward God. Then God can be recognized as the One who always already was desired and surmised, despite God's nameless hiding in obscurity.

Consideration of the *idea* of God, as somehow already present in the human mind, was the "method" adopted by Anselm, Bonaventure, Scotus, Descartes, Spinoza, Leibniz, and Hegel, when they dared affirm that this idea itself necessarily implies the existence of the God whose idea it is. The thought of that which absolutely surpasses all that is good, great, beautiful, being, and so on, refers to that which truly transcends all (other) beings and their totality in being good, great, beautiful, and being. But then its transcendence not only surpasses the universe *in thought;* the transcendent reality thought in the idea must also *be* and *exist* as such.

It is still controversial whether this argument is valid or invalid because of the homonymy of *being* as copula, essence, and existing, but in any case the idea itself grants the human mind an unlimited outreach. If this outreach does not make sense—that is, if the infinite to which it refers does not exist—or if it does exist, but only as unreachable, even then trust in it would not necessarily be impossible, but life would finish in disappointment. We would hope too much. However, if indeed the idea of God is not only a thought but also—and even primarily—the basic desire that constitutes, orients, motivates, and moves the human mode of existence as an incessant longing for the Infinite, would we then not recognize this Infinite as the desired and hoped for response?

That Jews, Christians, and Muslims believe in one, unique, infinite God, rarely has been the result of speculation. Most often, I guess, they believe, trust, and embrace its truth as the most welcome message that affects them as the most adequate, liberating, uplifting, consoling, and trustworthy response to the deepest longing that stirs their heart. Most of them have inherited this response from their family or surroundings; some have been touched suddenly or after a long search, but if a philosophical approach through reasoning and reflection has played any role at all, its contribution rarely surpasses the force of a confirmation.

This fact does not diminish the worth of a speculative approach to God. A civilization that is so fortunate as to harbor a strong philosophical tradition cannot refrain from translating its religious adventures and convictions into the language of its cogitation. What this means for Western culture can be studied on the basis of the documentation that more than two thousand years of Greek and post-Greek thinking have produced. How fruitful the amazing outburst of thought from Parmenides to Proclus and from Philo to Pascal was, can be shown from many perspectives—mythic, poetic, scientific, philosophical, political, and economic—but in the context of religion it is certainly the transformative adoption of ancient philosophy by the great Jewish, Christian, and Muslim thinkers that testifies to the illuminating and explicative power of that heritage, once it was integrated into the religious convictions that came from another origin: the origin of a trust that belonged to an irreducible alliance of God with humanity. An alliance is not the conclusion of an argument—faith is not a science—but it creates an infinite space and time, not only for prayer and meditation, but also for investigations and effective thought.

ATHEISM AND TRUST IN GOD

Being part of the human universe in active dedication to one's own life and all others' lives is certainly meaningful, but does it answer the most serious questions posed by our existence: Why do I—do we—exist? Why does the human universe exist? What is the meaning of it all? The question strikes us as urgent, if we realize that suffering, death, evil, and guilt threaten all meaning from the outset and possibly—probably—without end. However splendid and impressive the meaning of human endeavors and history may be, suffering spoils much of it and death destroys it inexorably if there is no meaning that transcends mortality, while evil corrupts the limited and provisional meanings we realize. If, however, human existence always already is related to the Infinite—in longing, seeking, and reaching out—and if this outreach may be interpreted as a return to which we are invited from the beginning, then it makes sense to trust that here and now and always—despite suffering, mortality, and guilt—the surpassing infinite, to which we are linked from the outset, encompasses and integrates the meanings that we realize in history.

Early atheism was experienced by its sympathizers as a daring rebellion against a dictatorial alliance of ecclesiastical and political powers. Finally humanity would free itself through a complete emancipation.

Now we will take our destiny into our own hands. Reason, Liberty, Humanity, Autonomy, History, Human Rights, Choice, and Democracy are the catchwords, whereas piety, prayer, humility, and edification are unmasked as debilitating.

Much of the attraction through which atheism has acquired adherents can be explained by the widespread—but incorrect—opinion that faith in God demands to be paid for by a loss of humanity, but attempts at proving the nonexistence of God were and are still rare. Such proofs are impossible, but many atheists point to several reasons for believing that the God of the believers does not, cannot, and must not exist. As we have seen, one of the strongest reasons coincides with a difficulty that arises also in the thinking of the faithful, but even more so in their lives. If God, the good, loving, and holy Creator, exists, how then is it possible that the universe abounds in suffering? The tragic aspect of nature and history seems incompatible with the claimed generosity of a creator. If we cannot or do not want to take refuge in a dualistic, hybrid, or cruel origin, it seems that we must deny a good, loving, all-creating God. At the risk of repeating some of what has already been said before, I would like to limit my response here to the following observations.

Why death and suffering belong to our natural condition and why humanity failed and continues to fail in maintaining its initial innocence, is a question that neither Job nor Jesus (who asked the question in dying[24]) have answered in any logically construable way. For us, citizens of the twenty-first century, the question has received gigantic dimensions because our daily news inundates us with information about the massive suffering and dying of innumerable babies, children, and other innocent boys, girls, men, and women, whereas so many perpetrators of the cruelest abuse and violence die in the safety of their wealthy mansions. It would be ridiculous and blasphemous to think that all who suffer deserve their suffering as appropriate punishment for their personal sins, and all other "explanations" that pair each morally bad action with an adequately penalizing pain distort too obviously the facts of history. Apparently our thinking stops when tragedy overwhelms our desperate questioning. Plato knew already that philosophy naturally hates tragedies, because they picture us as *inevitably* unjust, arrogant, murderous, and blasphemous. But even the theological attempts of Job's friends to justify his suffering failed in the face of God's response.[25] Not only did they ignore the tragic core of Job's lament, they also reduced the Lord to the dimensions of a petty moralist.

When believers do not close their senses to the ravaging cruelty of nature and history, they, like Job, have a hard time in seeking an answer to their lamentations. But what is better: to address—albeit in anger—an all-understanding and all-powerful Interlocutor, who grants provisional but mysterious answers, while delaying the conclusive ones, or to speak into a void, while joining the bitterness of all hearts without hope? Must the believers not recognize that their trust in the one providential God is not quite immune toward temptations of atheism? Would they completely deny that, once in a while, the anguish of being alone and forsaken is also murmuring in an obscure corner of their humiliated faith?[26]

ATHEIST PRAXIS

Atheists seem to lack an answer to the question of basic and ultimate trust. If they do not promote a substitute for the God of the monotheistic traditions by appealing to, for example, History, Nature, Life, or Fate, they tend to deny that the question itself is meaningful or to declare that believers are dreamers, "theologians," or too childish to cope with the reality. If they agree that human existence—and consequently the existence of a humanized and humanizable world—*must* have a meaning, they will claim that this meaning must be found within the boundaries of the human universe itself. This is a great incentive for scientific and philosophical examination and interpretation, and it is understandable that many atheists invest their intellectual energy in study and scholarship with a passion that is comparable to the passion of devout people who direct their thought toward the mysteries of their faith.

However, study and understanding do not constitute the most important or decisive requirement for a successful life. The meaning we are seeking must primarily be found in the living itself, that is, in the performance of the life that each individual, in relation with others within the history of humankind, is meant to practice. The question of praxis, in this sense, is much more urgent than any theoretical—philosophical, scientific, or theological—question. Indeed, theory can wait, but living a life does not permit delays. Life itself *is* the practical question and it has already given an answer by living on as soon as it is generated.

Atheists, as much as all believers, give an answer to the question of how to live by showing how they perform their lives. Once they have found out how to live (by trial and error, while accompanied by education), they can *also* try to formulate the mode or style and the habits or rules that should orient their lives and those of others. But their praxis cannot wait for textbooks or discussions about ethics.

Many ethicists have held that questions about "norms and values" cannot be solved unless a series of theoretical and normatively neutral questions have first been answered ("no *ought* without *is*" and "no *good* without a basic mode of being that is neither good nor bad"). Following that presupposition, believers as much as atheists have spent an enormous amount of time and energy on theoretical discussions about all sorts of subjects. With the startling exception of Kant, most modern philosophers have relegated questions of ethical, aesthetic, and religious behavior to secondary levels or to appendices of methodological, epistemological, and ontological treatises, which were deemed more fundamental. In chapter 6, we saw how Descartes postponed ethics by projecting it as part of the final stage, while he reserved most of his time for metaphysics and especially for physics. Hegel's system, which closes the epoch of the modern classics, confines the question of personal praxis to a subordinate portion of his treatises on right, and it is almost absent from his philosophy of religion. After Hegel, the development of a strictly personal praxis seems almost forgotten or treated as an outdated subject, which does not deserve the attention of creative thinkers. In the mean time, all philosophers, scientists, writers, doers, and livers continue to live a particular, in many respects similar, but at the same time strictly individual mode of life, even if they repeat or retrieve old ethical theories or do not bother to reflect on their own implicit assumptions.

However, if the confrontation between faith and the denial of God is an abyssal disagreement that shakes the foundations of our civilization, the urgency of a thorough discussion about the abyss is obscured by reducing it to a conflict between world visions without ethical consequences. If praxis is more basic than theories, and if the praxis of a singular or collective life is always concretized in a particular style or character and inspired by a distinct spirit, isn't a confrontation between God-less lives and faith-directed lives more important than a discussion between the theories to which the practitioners refer? A particular praxis does not always follow from or even fit into the theoretical conviction to which it appeals for its justification, but we can focus on the "spirit" that characterizes a typically atheist praxis and compare it with a praxis that is clearly animated by a religious inspiration. Such a comparison presupposes much preparation. A philosopher who would be learned and courageous enough to take on this task would need more assistance from historians, psychologists, and sociologists than I enjoy, but I can propose at least a few suggestions.

With regard to the conflict of atheism and Christianity, the last two centuries have offered us a variety of atheisms, but also several regimes that loudly boasted of being inspired by Christian principles. We have observed how Lenin's and Stalin's communism, Hitler's Nazism, Mussolini's Fascism, and Franco's version of dictatorial Catholicism have devastated Europe and how they have influenced the personal praxis of large populations, without, however, being able to transmute entirely the inherited traditions of Russia, Germany, Italy, or Spain, all of which did and, to a certain extent still do, contain many elements of their Christian heritage. It would therefore be as incorrect to identify atheism as such with any of the particular forms in which it has been realized as it would be to claim that Catholicism necessarily leads to a military dictatorship, as it did in Spain, or to pretend that the Christendom of any age was the most adequate expression of the spirit proclaimed by Jesus. However, one can affirm that Francis of Assisi was one obviously splendid—albeit particular—expression of that spirit. And, in any case, for the question of trust and distrust it makes a huge difference whether we talk about *orthopractical* or distorted concretizations of an ideal or belief.

Neither atheism nor Christianity have disappeared with the death of their corrupt, hypocritical, treacherous, violent, or antihuman implementations. It is, for example, an as yet unresolved question what kind of inspiration the "freedom" of the "democratic" West actually shows. Is the political praxis in our pseudodemocratic, hypocritical, greedy, consumerist, egoist, imperialist, and capitalist society less violent and more just, compassionate, forgiving, or charitable than its predecessors?

If the meaning of an individual life depends on the spirit and style of its praxis, what then can we say about the modes of living that are typical for an adequate praxis of atheism and a correct praxis of Christianity? This question presumes that, among the movements called atheist or Christian by their adherents, some at least present not only an explicit or implicit idea of human existence in the world, but also a practical ideal or orientation. Those Christian or atheist versions that do not bother about the style in which a life should be performed in order to be good are of no interest to a discussion on the question of how atheism and Christianity promote different forms of praxis and what consequences their difference might have for our trusting or distrusting them.

The genealogy of modern and postmodern atheism suggests that many of its versions show hostility and suspicion with regard to all religion-bound practices, while recommending trust in exclusively human endeavors, as supported by material, natural, and historical processes that would lead to a better—at once irreligious and humanist—way of life on earth. The modern preoccupation with a new foundation of human rights and the legal reordering of politics and economy was an eloquent example of the European and American switch in ethos that has busied many brilliant intellectuals during the last three or four centuries. It is an illustration of the postmedieval humanism that slowly replaced its Christian sources with merely human but universally valid foundations. Today, we see many people, especially young ones, who prefer to ignore religious questions while fervently dedicating themselves to humanitarian aid in the service of the poor and victimized, wherever they can be found. More than laws and rights, the needs of the violated and mistreated motivate the compassionate praxis of those who want to care for them. It is not necessary to reconstruct the role that Biblical or Koranic traditions still might play in their motivation, if we want to compare their inspiration to the dedication that inspires those of their colleagues who feel inspired by faith. Wouldn't such a comparison show a surprising affinity or even an (at least partial) identity, instead of the gap that seems to separate faith in God from the Godless humanitarianism of their colleagues in dedication to "the poor"?

Since atheism is not an institutionalized community with a list of orthodox articles and laws or principles, it is not possible to speak about *the* laws or virtues and vices of atheism. If, however, we simplify the question by seeing the phenomenon of compassionate dedication, just mentioned, as the core of contemporary atheism at its best or as the main paradigm of its secular humanism, it seems inevitable to confront this type of atheism with the core praxis of the still powerful ethico-religious tradition that unites Judaism, Christianity, and Islam.

Let me then begin with a reminder of the Christian praxis as it is recommended by the earliest testimonies of the Christian faith, after which we can ask whether, and to what extent, a certain form of atheism and the quintessential praxis of Christian faith express more affinity than a superficial look at them would discover.

CHRISTIAN PRAXIS

It is obviously impossible to give here a succinct theology of the many substyles of life in which Christianity has diversified its original message. But it is possible to transcribe and meditate on the summaries that are recorded in the Gospels. The following passage, for example, might speak for itself.

In one of the rare stories where Jesus and one of the scribes affirm a complete agreement,[27] the scribe asks Jesus: "Which is the first of all commandments?" The answer that Jesus gives is composed of two biblical quotes:

The first is: Hear Israel, the Lord is our God; the Lord is one; and you shall love the Lord your God with all your heart, and with all your soul, and with all your mind, and with all your strength.[28] The second is this: You shall love your neighbor as yourself.[29] There is no other commandment greater than these.

The scribe said to him: "Well said, teacher. You have said in truth that he is one and that there is no other but him; and that to love him with all your heart and with all your understanding and with all your strength, and to love your neighbor as yourself is more important than all burnt offerings and sacrifices."

Similar versions of this conversation are given in other gospels.[30] They are still more emphatic in stating that the two main commandments belong together and form one single commandment with two beloveds: God and the neighbor, no matter who he or she may be. In his version, Matthew even uses the word *equal* (*homoia*) to firmly state this unity:

Jesus replied: "Love the Lord your God with all your heart and with all your soul and with all your mind. This is the great and first commandment. And the second is like (*homoia*) it: Love your neighbor as yourself. All the Law and the Prophets depend on these two commandments."[31]

That loving God and loving all human others indeed coincide, is expressed in a parable about the last judgment, with which Jesus finished his teaching:

When the Son of Man comes in his glory . . . he will say to those at his right hand: "Come, you are blessed by my Father; take your inheritance, the kingdom prepared for you since the creation of the world. For I was hungry and you gave me something to eat. I was thirsty and you gave me something to drink. I was a stranger and you invited me. I needed clothes and you clothed me. I was sick and you looked after me. I was in prison and you came to visit me."[32]

When the persons whom he thus will recognize as the authentic heirs of his kingdom, then ask, "When did we see you hungry and feed you . . . ," the king will reply: "I tell you the truth, whatever you did for one of the least of these brothers or sisters of mine, you did for me."[33]

Even without entering into exegetical or theological discussions, it is clear that Jesus gives here a summary of the perfect praxis that makes a life good. The entire Bible is herewith declared to form one huge and ongoing commentary on the double command that defines a good life as a compassionate life, inspired by a wondrous love. The longing of our Desire cannot reach God, if, in loving God, it does not simultaneously embrace all humans, wherever they emerge.

However, the most amazing aspect of Jesus's answer is perhaps not the fact that he, in his way, says: "All you need [and all that the victims need] is love," but the affirmation that our love of the other *is equal (homoia) to* love of God. This equality has given birth to an immense number of commentaries, from Paul and Mark via a host of thinkers and poets to the prophets and mystics of all times. One could almost say that the entire history of theology is nothing else than an ongoing meditation on the omnipresent coincidence of God *and all humans* as the most lovable candidates for the love into which our originary desire unfolds.

If the worth of our lives depends on the extent to which our praxis will have been charitable, must we then not conclude that a final judgment about human lives cannot make an essential difference between those believers and deniers of God's existence who live for others? Both would do what, according to the believers, testifies to the presence of God in those who are charitably approached. Perhaps we could even go so far as to say that all charitable people perform a common religion, in which Love is celebrated as supreme inspiration and command. Believers would interpret *Love* as the name of God, while atheists would accept it as a name for the amazing Eros that inspires their dedication to other humans. Implicitly, both would serve a common passion for caring and compassion in the name of a power that surpasses the multiplicity of egocentric selves.

GUILT AND PARDON

When we talk about praxis and behavior, it is almost inevitable that, at a certain moment, we stumble on our missteps and wrongdoings. More than evil in the form of sicknesses, death and suffering from other natural and social disasters, historical events, and personal damages, we should and we do regret the forms of evil we ourselves perpetrate. Who can deliver us from the guilt we have accumulated at so many occasions of our lives? Who is able to take my and our guilt away?

The facts of the past cannot be erased, but their meaning can still change depending on their follow-up or their retrieval in an as yet unpredictable future. But even if it is possible to make up for the harm we did, do humans possess enough power to forgive what made the harm malevolent, hateful, and often irreparable? If the harm can be compensated to a certain extent, how then can I be forgiven, purified, or renewed by persons who have already died? Can anyone else replace them in pardoning me? Must I remain in debt and guilty forever? I recognize my failures and omissions as bad and consequently also as harming me. I feel the humiliation they cause me after the fact, and I must learn how to bear with the self-caused shame and blame they left behind in me. Who can deliver me from this burden and how can I repair the harm to others and myself that I have caused?

Persons who face each other can try to make up for wrongdoing by restitution, by giving a gift, or by charitable acts, although a true erasure of one's fault would demand a more creative power to wash away the stain that is left or to rebuild in the past what has been destroyed. If the harmed other is no longer reachable, I am alone with my guilt. And if this guilt grows monstrously, how can I bear with it without hating myself or becoming mad?

The temptation is great to reduce one's missteps as much as possible by repressing or forgetting them or by interpreting them as well-meant and innocent—or, if need be, as stupid—gestures, but such a reduction leads to lying and inauthenticity, which makes things only more ugly.

Some of those who believe in the possibility of keeping a singular life within the walls of their egoism consider the possibility of pardoning oneself, but that seems a presumptuous idea. Perhaps they mean that I not only must learn how to cope with the blame I deserve and the shame that fills my conscience, but also purify and renew my attitude to start a better period of life. But wanting to be at the same time culprit and judge, while forgiving me in the name of the harmed or dead victim—without giving her a chance to refuse—seems a preposterous inflation of ego's sovereignty. Usurping a brand new innocence for myself, while leaving the wounded to their pains and the murdered to dust—is that not a complete reversal of begging pardon?

One cannot live peacefully after committing terrible harm to others. Guilt and inner shame, more than external blame, compress the murderer's self-consciousness and narrow its imprisonment in deepest solitude. Anguish and dread replace light and liberty; one feels no longer at home in oneself, and it becomes difficult to believe in being welcome in the homes of others.

It is not death or dying that causes the deepest *angst.* The guilt that follows murder, abuse, contempt, or vilification is much worse. Even lesser misdeeds have a depressing effect. It is therefore necessary to know how one can be freed from guilt or, if that is not possible, how we can live with it, while at least keeping some rest of innocence alive. But what or whom can we trust in longing for purification and recovery?

Trust in God, the creator, is also trust in God as renewer of human lives. In all cultures, major crimes have been associated with the need for reconciliation with the sacred forces that are offended. Conversion and purification are needed. In Judaism, Christianity, and Islam, forgiveness of sins is always related to the divine source of all charity, which includes the deepest respect for sanctity, justice, compassion, forgiving, and peace. If the highest form of love is the love of one's enemy, it is also credible that God forgives in a divine way, which encompasses radical purification and sanctification, and even a rebirth and reflourishing of the life and the splendor that were destroyed.

Such forgiveness includes a restructuring of the pardoned sinner, and a rebeginning of benevolent praxis; a real renaissance—even a recreation—of lost glory. The message of faith is simple: genuine conversion to God is crowned by resurrection. If hope and trust are possible, this is not because of any egoic sovereignty, but only thanks to a sovereign forgiving that reveals the creator as savior and redeemer. But theology needs centuries to meditate on the mysteries involved in the overcoming of the greatest evil: sin.

What can atheism say and do about crimes, guilt, pardon, and conversion? All these words must be secularized to fit a Godless treatise, if such is possible, about trust and distrust in their most basic and ultimate dimension. The perspective from which moral and social evils are approached is then enclosed within the limitations of a nonsacred but cosmic and historical temporality. The questions asked within this horizon are similar to the questions formulated above: How can we cope with individual and collective evils? Can we trust that they may be overcome and redeemed? Guilty individuals will long for liberation from their conscience's anguish and desolation, but their experience of guilt and liberation does not include acknowledged relations with sacred realities beyond the human universe. Not only do they, too, want to be forgiven for actions that haunt their memory; they also desire to become better, more noble, humane, authentic, dedicated, loving, courageous, and, in general, more virtuous. Instead of seeking intimacy with God, they concentrate, like their religious colleagues and friends, on good relationships with their family, friends, and neighbors, while contributing to movements that promise individual and collective progress. Since humanity itself forms the widest horizon of any nonidolatrous atheism, the basic trust of its adherents is motivated by a desire to make the human condition less egoist, criminal, unjust, corrupt, and more pacific, friendly, generous, compassionate, loving, and lovable.

Does this mean that the praxis of the best atheists coincides with the praxis of the best Christians? If it is not necessary to have personally encountered God or Christ in order to be associated with the originary Love, the answer could be affirmative. Some—or many—of those who seem to stay outside, are more inside than some or many who assume that they live inside. However, there must be differences. Not only does religious devotion elicit a different economy of affections and motivations than an exclusively ethical one, the difference between an exclusively temporal and an eternal perspective separates two kinds of experience, width, and expectation. Certainly, true dedication to the advancement of humanity in peace and justice may rely on the trust that history goes on and that our efforts will result in better epochs than the murderous one in which we live, but this trust is not guaranteed at all, and even if it is a plausible and necessary element of our hope, it does not answer the most intimate Desire of the millions who are dying before the desired world will have been realized.

If neither God nor friendly gods exist and love us, we are too desirous to accept this wounded and mortal universe as our final destination. Eschatological trust is indispensable to maintain our human—quite human—hope.

AGNOSTIC SUSPENSION AND TRUST IN LOVING HOPE

Outside of the monotheist traditions, today's main "religious" trend seems to be an agnostic attitude, which does not decide for or against faith in God, because it does not see convincing reasons that would justify either decision. Especially among young intellectuals—whether or not educated in a religious milieu—the sacred stories about Israel, Jesus and his followers, and the liturgies of the churches seem to have lost much of their attraction. Apparently, these stories have not been told very well, not even well enough to awaken much desire for a serious exploration of a splendid past. Not only philosophical and scientific attacks, but also many unenlightened words and immoral actions of bishops, priests, and bureaucrats have undermined the authority of the Church they represent, while the explanations of theologians are widely perceived as too outdated or arcane to excite a passion for serious contemplation. During a few decades of the last century, young intellectuals looked eastward for religious wisdom, but the trend of traveling to India for spiritual enlightenment seems to be over. Many young and adult people feel at ease without belonging to an explicit religious movement, although a certain hunger for spiritual food is not entirely dead, if I may trust my experience with students who expect more from philosophy than training in sophisticated forms of reasoning. On both sides of the ocean, however, few academics seem troubled by dramatic struggles for or against religion, belief in God, or atheism. Has the entire dimension of existential depth vanished without leaving regret or pain? Has the religious dimension been emptied of longing and desire?

The discovery of new adventures and new forms of dedication, such as immersion in the third world, feminism, animal rights, and ecological concerns may be the new catalysts of the pathos that former generations energized in their sense of mission, but even young philosophers are seldom fascinated or personally bothered by the most profound texts of the greatest thinkers, often dismissed as "speculative" or "metaphysical." Their rather untormented, though often puzzled, life expresses trust, though it is accompanied by many—especially political—forms of distrust. But trust and distrust in what? If the question of God's existence in their lives is bracketed and most often silenced or postponed, their trust must be based on something else. In this sense their mood shows some affinity with the trust of nonmilitant atheists. Unless, of course, their assurance testifies silently to a half- or unconscious kind of anchoring in a secret that functions as incognito of God. Some of today's agnostics indeed point to a core in themselves that resists all violation, comparable perhaps to a sacred mystery that must be respected at any cost. Others seem to be content with being part of the world's history of discovery and production, or they embrace life's own demands without withdrawing from it for solitary reflexivity, whereas those who are not afraid of metaphysics might consider being, beauty or goodness themselves to be the true sources of meaning.

Since death is inexorable, such forms of trust remind us that we should be modest: "Accept your life, as tied to this particular history; it offers enough exciting opportunities of (finite) meaning! Do not indulge in longing for eternity or infinite dimensions of making sense! To be desirous of the Absolute is an illusion, good for myths and dramatization, but it is not 'a natural desire,' despite the affirmations of all great philosophers from Plato, Aristotle, and Plotinus on."[34]

The way in which I try to roughly sketch here a few answers that are given to the question about trust is probably too explicit, because the question itself is not often experienced as very urgent. However, there is a remarkable difference between at least a certain part of this generation and former ones. If we bracket those young adults who want to make millions and have a lot of fun, but otherwise hardly differ from standard adaptations of former generations, a large group distinguishes itself by impressive dedication to poor, sick, destitute, threatened, or victimized people at home and abroad. The way in which Doctors Without Borders, Peace Corps, and many other public and private associations answer the inevitable question of how to live meaningfully is not primarily adhesion to a particular creed, followed by meditation, theological studies, and pastoral work. Their practical forms of dedication are in many respects similar to the practices that are recommended by great religious traditions about justice, charity, compassion, and solidarity. The implicit message of their dedication seems to be: "This kind of existing for others makes sense. Be convinced that working for the poor, including the difficulties and pains it involves, grants meaning to their and your own lives!"

That such is the message of their remarkable praxis seems confirmed by the avidity with which many representatives of this generation receive the writings of Emmanuel Levinas. With or without religion, a surprising number of his readers have recognized the human "face" as a clear and irrefutable revelation of the other's vulnerable but inviolable dignity. It is your face, which imposes the command of all commands on me, who is regarded by it. Don't we observe here an amazing rediscovery, on a cosmopolitan scale, of the beatitudes within and without the framework of organized religions? Levinas seems to be right in calling the face of the Other a *revelation* and an *epiphany*, because the command that your face addresses to me *is* the visibility of a call that transcends your and my own capacity.[35] Should we then not recognize this as a call through which God protects everyone's dignity by signifying to every me who encounters *You* that I must love *You* (which implies—as I would like to add—that likewise I, as other for any you, am also protected and loved by God). If we can trust this all-embracing love, dedication to others coincides with a meaningful enactment of one's own existence. Trust in this coincidence then is identical with trusting that the Infinite reveals itself by creating and saving all humans out of a divine love that gathers them—not only by virtue of its own grace, but also by way of their human love.

If the face is a sign of God's facing humans, we might also ask whether perhaps all manifestations of being as such must be understood as a manner of addressing, revealing, targeting, calling, challenging, and summoning, which motivates the addressees to wonder, trust, obedience, service, admiration, gratitude, and hope. As hiding a divine presence, being itself would then greet and awaken us through a million beings to a responsive attitude of appreciation and enjoyment. By accepting existence and personal unicity, including the pain and suffering that go with it, we are then capable of living in a way that makes sense. Being as a giving gift would then be trustably eloquent, or, as Scripture's poetic story about creation calls it, human existence would be a good, very good, and trustworthy metaphor, image, symbol, and sacrament of God's creative and meaning-granting *Word.*

NOTES

INTRODUCTION

1. Cf. Martin Heidegger, *Being and Time,* §§ 40 and 52–53, trans. Joan Stambaugh (Albany, N.Y.: SUNY Press, 1996), 172–177, 236–246; and Emmanuel Levinas, *De l'existence à l'existant* (Paris: Vrin, 1990), 93–105.

2. Cf. chapter 8 of this volume.

1. TRUST

1. For more on the contrast between dative and objectifying acts, see chapter 2.

2. Chapter 2 continues this preliminary analysis of entrusting.

3. Cf. *Nicom. Ethics,* I, 12–III, 5 (1101 b10–1115 a5). Cf. also Paul Ricoeur, *Philosophie de la Volonté I: Le volontaire et l'involontaire* (Paris: Aubier, 1949), 453–456, for a summary of the conclusions.

4. Trust and distrust are certainly important topics in any analysis of the fundamental relations between morality and contractual law.

5. Cf. Plato, *Politeia* IX, 572b–590a.

6. The following chapter proposes a more detailed analysis of one major example of vertical trust, whereas chapter 3 (on trust in politics) offers some precisions regarding horizontal trust.

7. As Hegel implies in chapter 3 of *Phänomenologie des Geistes* (vol. 3 of G. W. F. Hegel, *Werke* [Frankfurt am Main: Suhrkamp, 1970]).

2. ENTRUSTING

1. See Adriaan T. Peperzak, *Elements of Ethics* (Stanford, Calif.: Stanford University Press, 2004), 56–72.

2. Ibid., 98–175.

3. Cf. Descartes, *Discours de la Méthode,* AT VI, 62: "maîtres et possesseurs de la nature"; and chapters 4 and 6 of this book.

3. TRUST AND SOCIETY

1. In *Politica* I, 1 (1252 a 1), Aristotle uses the word *koinonia* (commonness), which Aquinas translates as *societas.* Here I use both *community* and *society* as generic names for all forms of togetherness that have at least some specific—albeit weak—unity.

2. Which one does *not* lose but, on the contrary, liberates by entrusting one's willing to an *infinite* Benevolence, if this exists.

3. If this book—against my intention—overemphasizes the role of our receptivity, instead of once more *prolonging* two hundred years of jubilation about individual choice, liberty, and originality, my excuse would be that—due to a widespread overrating of liberty and choice—acceptance, gratitude, loyalty, and patience are still much too little appreciated.

4. *Values* seems to be the most overused and worn-out expression for evoking what formerly was called morally or ethically *good.* It is a favorite expression in mission statements of universities; but accurate speakers or writers avoid it, because it is much too vague to say anything interesting about the *kind* of quality one wants to recommend. Is it more than a stopgap, which we can use to avoid a serious discussion about fundamental questions of ethics and metaphysics, such as, What do we mean, when we call someone or something *good* (or *bad*)?

5. The translation of *politeia* (that is, political constitution) by "republic" is extremely misleading, because it wrongly suggests that all the constitutions Plato presents, would have a republican form. The Latin expression *res publica* (that is, the *common entity,* whose common good must guarantee the well-being of all citizens *and* their common interest) does not imply any particular form of government.

6. See Adriaan Peperzak, *Modern Freedom. Hegel's Legal, Moral, and Political Philosophy* (Dordrecht: Springer, 2001), esp. 499–504, 512–521.

7. Cf. *Platonic Transformations* (Oxford: Rowman and Littlefield, 1997), 19–56.

8. Cf. *Politeia,* books VIII and IX.

9. By putting the emphasis on sincerity as an essential feature of trustworthiness, we could, for instance, focus on the truth-loving character of an ideal community. We would then ask: Do the authorities often lie to us? Are their plans, budgets, and decisions transparent? Is it a habit of the citizens to cheat,

for example, while trading with one another or in filling out their tax forms? Is lying tolerated, liked, recommended by the most influential or the majority of citizens? And so on. That lying is the beginning of corruption does not need complicated arguments. It is too obvious that egoism hides behind insincerity. Not all lying is egoist, however, because there are violent states, where judicious forms of lying in dire circumstances are the only way to realize altruistic forms of protection to be effective. Imagine telling the truth about hiding a completely innocent person, when asked about his whereabouts by a monstrous regime!

4. COUNTING ON NATURE

1. Cf. chapter 1, on the contrast between dative and objective modes of approaching and being-given.

2. See chapter 6 for a sketch of the modern framework.

5. SELF-CONFIDENCE

1. Cf. the dictum of Solon, which Aristotle quotes in his *Nichomachean Ethics* I, 10 (1100a 11–12): "Look at the end." If this is the answer to the question of whether a particular life can be called *eudaimōn*, only certain dead persons can be called happy.

2. Cf. Aristotle, *Nichomachean Ethics*, I, 7 (1097 b 25): *to ergon tou anthrōpou* (the essentially human work).

3. Cf. Adriaan Peperzak, *Elements of Ethics* (Stanford, Calif.: Stanford University Press, 2004), 73–97.

6. TRUST IN PHILOSOPHY

1. In using the words *science* and *scientific* to describe Descartes's ideal of philosophy, I follow his (and the medieval) use of the word "science" (*scientia*) as encompassing what *we* distinguish as philosophy *and* the sciences.

2. Cf., Adriaan Peperzak, *The Quest for Meaning: Friends of Wisdom from Plato to Levinas* (New York: Fordham University Press, 2003), 123–148.

3. René Descartes, *Discours de la Méthode*, pt. 6, AT VI, 22–23. For further commentary, see "Life, Science, and Wisdom According to Descartes," in *The Quest for Meaning*, 123–148.

4. Cf. Adriaan Peperzak, *Thinking: From Solitude to Dialogue and Contemplation* (New York: Fordham University Press, 2006), 1–22, 131–136.

5. G. W. F. Hegel, *Gesammelte Werke* (Hamburg, Felix Meiner, 1995), 18:18.

7. TRUST IN SEARCH OF INSIGHT

1. Cf. Adriaan Peperzak, "Unendlichkeit zwischen Hegel und Levinas," in *Unendlichkeit im Deutschen Idealismus,* ed. Francesca Menegoni and Luca Illetterati (Stuttgart: Klett-Cotta, 2004), 186–208.

2. Cf. Gregory of Nyssa, *The Life of Moses,* II, n. 163.

3. In a nonsynthetic sense, which transcends any synthesis or totality.

4. Cf. Aristotle, *Metaphysics,* XII, 7 (1072 b3–4).

5. *Fides quaerens intellectum* is the title of Anselm of Canterbury's small book that is better known under the subtitle *Proslogion.* The formula is an excellent summary of the philosophical/theological method practiced by Augustine and more than one thousand years of Augustinianism. See, for example, the translation of Anselm's *Proslogion* by Thomas Williams, (Indianapolis, Ind.: Hackett, 1995).

8. TRUST IN GOD OR THE UNIVERSE?

1. *Religion* here can be understood in both the restricted sense of the local and the world religions and in the very broad sense sometimes used in the present book, which includes the level of ultimate questions, as they are posed by atheists. If the last meaning is emphasized, it will be indicated clearly enough to prevent equivocation.

2. History is the collective adventure of cultural encounters, shifts, collisions, harmonizations, and so on.

3. St. Augustine, De Civitate Dei, XIX, 1, 3: *Nulla est homini causa philosophandi nisi ut beatus sit* ("the only reason for anybody to practice philosophy is the desire to be happy").

4. Cf. chapter 4 of Adriaan Peperzak, *Elements of Ethics* (Stanford, Calif.: Stanford University Press, 2004).

5. Cf. Martin Heidegger, *Sein und Zeit,* §§ 50–53.

6. The lack or privation (*privation boni*), which figures in the definition of evil since Greek antiquity, is not a simple absence but the qualified absence or no-show of a good whose presence *ought* to be realized, present, showing up, coming, or becoming. Evil is never an initial form of being, becoming, showing, doing, acting, enjoying. It is not original, not a principle, and it is neither created nor creative, but always secondary: perverting, corrupting, destructive, hostile, diminishing, weakening, emptying; smoke, vanity, antidivine—and thus antihuman, antilife, and anticosmos.

7. Cf. chapters 3–5.

8. Cf. Genesis 2:4–3:24.

9. Even Descartes interrupted his metaphysical meditations by terminating the third day with a prayer from the heart: he takes time to "consider, admire, and adore the *incomparable* beauty of this [God's] immense light, at least as much as the strength of my spirit, somehow blinded by it, permits me to do so." (AT VII, 42).

10. Cf. Paul Ricoeur, *Finitude et culpabilité,* vol. 2: *La symbolique du mal* (Paris: Aubier, 1960), 218–260.

11. Genesis 1:1–2:3.

12. Genesis 2:4–3:24.

13. Genesis 4:1–24.

14. Genesis 3:1–4, 13–15.

15. This statement presupposes the *noncompetitive,* but infinitely confirmative and originary coincidence of loving God and loving one's neighbors.

16. As it is done in this chapter, which must therefore be read in connection with the descriptions of the trustworthy aspects of the universe that were given in part 2.

17. Just as *religion,* the word *faith* can be used in a more restricted or a broader sense. I focus here on the faith of Christians, Jews, and Muslims, but analogically similar statements are valid with respect to nonmonotheist religions and to a certain extent also, I think, of atheist and agnostic forms of ultimate trust.

18. Cf. Joachim Ritter, ed., *Historisches Wörterbuch der Philosophie,* vol. 1 (Darmstadt: Wissenschaftliche Buchgesellschaft, 1971), col. 957–960; and Ernst Curtius, *European Literature and the Latin Middle Ages,* trans. Willard R. Trask (New York: Harpers & Row, 1963), 319–332.

19. Cf. Adriaan Peperzak, "Religion after Onto-Theo-Logy?" in *Philosophy between Faith and Theology* (Notre Dame, Ind.: University of Notre Dame Press, 2005), chap. 7 (85–102): "Retrieving Onto-Theo-Logy."

20. As a reminder, I want to stress again that my focusing on the faith of Christians is not motivated by any disrespect with regard to other religions but only by my own greater familiarity with the Christian tradition. Belonging to the Church does not forbid but, on the contrary, fosters the hope that our various histories through many roads may progressively converge into a colorful and well-styled but peacefully united humanity.

21. To what extent the distinction between *believing in* and *believing that,* as it is explained here, is also valid for all or some of the other religions is beyond the scope of this book. Neither will I thematize the parallel between *believing that* and *believing about,* on the one hand, in contrast with *believing in* and *speaking* (or answering) *to,* on the other. While writing about religion, faith, theology,

and their relation to philosophy and the sciences, I have taken Christianity as my main paradigm, while, at the same time, trying to find formulations that could be recognized as analogically more or less applicable to other ways of seeking God.

22. Cf. Ps 31:5 and Lk 23:46.

23. If the word *theism* expresses one of several philosophical doctrines (and what else could it mean if it is not only an ideology?), God cannot be found in theism. In this sense none of the classics of onto-theo-logy is therefore a *theist.* Trust or belief in God is non-"a-*theist*" in its own way, whereas many (most?) forms of modern and postmodern atheism focus on a caricature that they equally call "God," while claiming its nonexistence.

24. Mk 15:34.

25. Cf. Job 38:1–41:26.

26. For a classical example of the way in which the problem of evil and suffering is connected with the existence of God by one of the great modern philosophers, Leibniz, see Adriaan Peperzak, *The Quest for Meaning* (New York: Fordham University Press, 2003), 170–194.

27. Mark 12:28–34.

28. Quoted from Deuteronomy 6:4–5.

29. Quoted from Leviticus 19:18.

30. Cf. Matthew 22:34–40 and Luke 20:27–38.

31. Matthew 22:37–40.

32. Matthew 25:31, 34–36.

33. Matthew 25: 37, 40–41.

34. The writer of these lines, imagined by me, who put these words in his mouth, considers *Eros* to be a primary condition and norm of all "great" philosophy. I tried to justify his conviction in several retrievals of Plato's ascent to the Good-and-Beautiful. Cf. my *Platonic Transformations: With and after Hegel, Heidegger, and Levinas* (New York: Rowman and Littlefield, 1997), 127–150, 205–226; *Elements of Ethics* (Stanford, Calif.: Stanford University Press, 2004), 73–97; and *Savoir et Sagesse* (Paris: Presses Universitaires de France, 2011), 47–72.

35. For a more detailed justification of this summary of Levinas's analysis of facing and being faced, *see* Emmanuel Levinas, *Totality and Infinity: An Essay on Exteriority* (Pittsburgh, Penn.: Duquesne University Press, 1969), 187–204.

INDEX